The Train Doesn't Stop Here Any More

The Train Doesn't Stop Here Any More

An Illustrated History of Railway Stations in Canada

Ron Brown

broadview press

Cataloguing in Publication Data

Brown, Ron, 1945-
The train doesn't stop here any more

ISBN 0-921149-84-0

1. Railroads — Canada — Stations — History
2. Railroads — Canada — Stations — Pictoral Works.
I. Title.

TF302.C3B7 1991   385'.314'0971   C91-094960-3

The publisher gratefully acknowledges the assistance of the
Ontario Arts Council.

Unless otherwise noted, photographs are by
the author.

in Canada: in the US:
broadview press   **broadview press**
P.O. Box 1243   269 Portage Rd.
Peterborough, Ontario   Lewiston, NY
K9J 7H5   14092

Front cover background: Glenbow Archives.

Front cover foreground (photo by the author): Fernie, B.C. This CPR station was completed in 1908, two previous stations having been destroyed by fire. It is the last remaining class A station along the Crowsnest Pass branch line. Although the train doesn't stop here any more, the Fernie District Arts Council has recently restored the structure as a heritage building housing a restaurant, theatre, gallery, and fine arts studios.

Title Page: CP Corporate Archives (Schreiber, Ontario).

Contents

*This book is dedicated to the
memory of my late father,
Arnold Brown.
His inspiration lives.*

Acknowledgements

In most book acknowledgement sections, authors conclude with "those whose names are too numerous to mention". The folks whose names follow generously shared with me their time, their information, their memories, their photographs and their companionship, and, although numerous, they deserve mention. They are:

Darryl Allan, Fort Frances Museum, Fort Frances, Ontario
Allan Anderson, Tottenham, Ontario
Len Appleyard, Richmond Hill, Ontario
T.M. Bate, CN Community Affairs, Winnipeg, Manitoba
Nancy Battet, CP Archives, Montreal, Quebec
Mrs Ollie Bertie, Taber, Alberta
Rejean Blais, VIA Atlantic, Moncton, New Brunswick
Bill Bobek, MuchMusic, Toronto, Ontario
Jean Roche Boivin, Q.C., VIA, Montreal, Quebec
Brendan Carruthers, Travel Manitoba
Andre Bolduc, Quebec Ministre des Transports, Montreal, Quebec
Ernie Boyd, Ompah, Ontario
Helena Campbell, Simcoe, Ontario
The Venerable A.E.L. Caulfield, Archdeacon Emeritus, Saint John, New Brunswick
Clayton D. Cook, Lethbridge, Newfoundland
Charles Cooper, Toronto, Ontario
Steve Dale, Environment Canada, Parks Service
Russ Davey, YMCA Archives, Orillia, Ontario
Penny Demmings, Tourism New Brunswick
Ed Emery, Toronto, Ontario
L.J. Fleece, former archivist, Ontario Northland Railway, North Bay, Ontario
Bill Foster, Ottawa, Ontario
Lawrence Friend, Environment Canada, Ottawa
Beth Gaffney, Regina, Saskatchewan
Hilda Geddes, Snow Road, Ontario
Ralph Geddes, Mississippi Station, Ontario
Ray Gilchrist, Lethbridge, Alberta
Anne Haines, Kelligrews, Newfoundland
Bill Hamilton, Nepean, Ontario
Mr. Ed Holmes, Keewatin, Ontario
Isabel Hill, Elphin, Ontario
F.A. Howard-Gibbon, Prince George, British Columbia
Norm Jaerling, Director of Economic Development, White River, Ontario
Mrs. P. Johnson, Lethbridge, Alberta
Kingsley Kennedy, Dunrobin, Ontario
Shane Kennedy, Ottawa, Ontario
Al and Jean Kincaid, Avonlea, Saskatchewan

Les Kozma, Edmonton, Alberta
Walter Long, Fredericton, New Brunswick
Doug MacKrenzie, CN Trainmaster, Capreol, Ontario
Marisa Lacaria, CN, Toronto, Ontario
Mrs. Queen Maloney, Bay Bulls, Newfoundland
Mrs. F.J. Manning, Reston, Manitoba
K.P. Markoff, CN Community Affairs, Edmonton, Alberta
Gwen Martin, Fredericton, New Brunswick
Janet Martin, Environment Canada, Parks Service, Ottawa
Stephen McIntosh, CN Public Affairs, Moncton, New Brunswick
M. McKenzie, VIA, Vancouver, British Columbia
Mr. Homer McClain, Lethbridge, Alberta
Donalda McClure, Chesley, Ontario
Russ McMillen, National Film Board of Canada, Toronto, Ontario
Richard Moorhouse, Ontario Ministry of Culture and Communication, Toronto, Ontario
Mrs Mary O'Malley, Charlottetown, Prince Edward Island
J. O'Hara, Canadian Transport Commission, Ottawa, Ontario
Lorne.C. Perry, Vice President, CN Advertising, Montreal, Quebec
A.P. Rennie, Manager Public Affairs, CN, Edmonton, Alberta
Connie Romani, CN Public Affairs, Montreal, Quebec
Mr David C. Rossiter, Lethbridge, Alberta
Maureen Rourke, Hill and Knowlton Communications, Toronto, Ontario
B.C. Scott, CP Public Relations, Montreal, Quebec
Muriel J. Shepherd, Lethbridge, Alberta
Mrs Nan Sheppard, Simcoe, Ontario
Pat Simpson, Burlington, Ontario
Thomas G. Smith, GO Transit, Toronto, Ontario
Dave Spaulding, East York, Ontario
Mrs Margery Spearin, Rivers, Manitoba
Alice E. Takacs, Lethbridge, Alberta
Margo Teasdale, Ontario Ministry of Culture and Communications, Toronto, Ontario
Peter Tiedemann, Toronto, Ontario
Rick Thompson, Lethbridge, Alberta
Paul Thurston, CP Public Relations, Toronto, Ontario
Mr. John H. Treloar, Rivers, Manitoba
Nary Ada Upstone, Prince Edward Island Tourism, Charlottetown, Prince Edward Island
Robert Vaughan, Smiths Falls Railway Museum Association, Smiths Falls, Ontario
Joseph S. White, Taylor, Michigan
James Wood, MuchMusic, Toronto, Ontario
Clayton Workman, Bruce Mines, Ontario
Donna Zuchlinski, Ontario Film Development Corporation, Toronto, Ontario

And the many railway employees, whose names I failed to take but from whom I gleaned invaluable items for the book. Thanks too to the Ontario Arts Council and to the following archives, libraries and museums and other sources of photographs and information:

National Archives of Canada, Picture Collection, Map Collection and Government Records
Ontario Archives
Algonquin Park Museum
Glenbow Museum Archives
Saskatchewan Archives Board
Canpress

Medicine hat News
Metro Toronto Library, Baldwin Room, and Arts Department
City of Vancouver Archives
British Columbia Archives
Norwich and District Historical Society
The Oil Museum of Canada
Lake of the Woods Museum
St Lawrence Parks Commission
Lennox and Addington County Museum
Notman Photographic Archives, McCord Museum
Gravenhurst Archives Committee
Heritage Scarborough
Yukon Tourism, Heritage Branch
County of Bruce Museum
Provincial Archives of Alberta
Provincial Archives, Manitoba Culture, Heritage and Recreation
CN Photo Library and Reference Library
CP Corporate Archives
City of Ottawa Archives
Victoria City Archives
Provincial Archives of Newfoundland and Labrador
City of Toronto Archives
Thunder Bay Museum
Muskoka Pioneer Museum
London Public Library
Hamilton Public Library
Todmorden Mills Historic Park Archives, East York
Sudbury Public Library
Archives Nationales du Quebec
Provincial Archives of New Brunswick
Provincial Archives of Prince Edward Island
McMichael Canadian Collection
Ontario Northland Railway Archives

I would like to thank particularly Gordon Wagar of Oro Station, Ontario, for kindly reading selected sections of the manuscript and offering his comments.

Finally, thanks to my ever patient family, June, Jeri and Ria for putting up with a lot of station hunts.

1ST PASSENGER TRAIN
REACHED CALGARY
AUG, 1883.

C.P. RAILWAY STATION
CALGARY. 1884.
ERNEST BROWN 813A
COPYRIGHT.

WOOD BURNING
ENGINE, NO. 144.

What is a Station?

Provincial Archives of Alberta B 3152

Bellis Station, located in the Ukrainian Heritage Park east of Edmonton, Alberta, has been preserved and restored to recreate the station in its heyday. Shown here is the agent's office.

(opposite) The CPR station, Calgary, 1894.

Confusion often exists between the terms "station" and "depot." As defined in railway timetables, a station is a stopping place and need not be a structure. In fact, it may be nothing more than a siding, a platform, or a mail hook. "Depot," an American term, refers to the building itself. Nevertheless, in Canada the word "station" popularly refers to that wonderful old building, with its semaphore, its bay window, its platform, and its waiting room full of memories.

Whatever it was called, the station was vital for train operations and for customers. On the operational side, it housed offices for administrators, and provided sidings and yards for rolling stock, maintenance and fuel for the locomotives, equipment for the orderly movement of trains, and shelter and food for the train crews. To customers the station was where they shipped parcels, bought money orders, or sent telegrams; where they picked up their mail or loaded their farm produce; where they bought their tickets for a trip around the world or just to the next town; and where they awaited the train that would take them there. They could even eat at the station.

Clearly, a station could be many things, and the number of functions it had determined what kind of station it was. A station could range from something as simple as shelter for passengers with a platform for freight and a mail crane, to a large urban palace with everything from executive suites to shoe-shine stands. In between were the divisional stations, and the most common of all, the way stations.

The Country Stations

It is the way stations, or operator stations, that most Canadians remember. Nearly every town, after all, had one. Outside they remember the wooden semaphores perched at various angles, the water tank looming over the track, the milk cans and the egg crates piled high on the platform, the dark green canvas bags bulging with mail resting on the wagon. And they remember the waiting room with its smell of kerosene and the sound of the ticking clock.

Because so much was packed into the little buildings, the layout was critical. All services had to be arranged within the building so that passengers, freight, and mail were all handy to the agent. And always within reach were the train order crank, the typewriter, and the telegraph key, all indispensable for train movement.

(right) The Port Stanley Terminal railway station displays the early style of train order board. When the board was parallel to the track, it was a "clear board" and the engineer could proceed without stopping. When the board was perpendicular to the track, the engineer had to stop. Atop the spindle were red and green glass covers in front of a lamp. When the board was in the stop position, the red glass covered the lamp; the "clear board" placed the green glass before the lamp.

(far right) A semaphore at Kleinberg, Ontario.

The Agent's Office

The heart of the operation was the agent's office, located in the centre. A bay window protruded over the platform to allow him to see down the track and keep his eye on the platform. In the agent's office, set into the bay window, stood a large oak desk with typewriter, telephone, and piles of forms everywhere. Also on the desk was the all-important telegraph key. Here the information clattered through from the dispatcher's office to let the agent know when a train was on the way. To one side of the office was the ticket window, barred to discourage thieves, where passengers would buy their tickets or just come to chat. On the other side was the entrance to the freight room, where express parcels, mail, and freight waited beside the milk cans and egg crates for shipment to the next town. Each section had separate doors on to the platform and usually separate entrances from the street. Behind the office was

the door that lead to the agent's quarters.

In remoter locations where no permanent settlement had sprung up by the track, the "station" was often a house for the operator and his equipment. In such areas section houses sometimes doubled as stations.

The Wooden Arms

Just outside the agent's office were the wooden arms, one red and one green, poised at various angles from a pole above or beside the bay window. These arms were the semaphores; they gave the locomotive engineer his instructions to stop or to proceed without stopping.

Canada's first stations had no train order boards. Engineers were required to stop at each station and sign for orders. To reduce unnecessary stops, the railways placed a ball on top of a pole before the station to give the engineer permission to continue full speed ahead. The term "highballing" originated

with this device and has remained in the railway lexicon ever since.

The first order boards were, as the name implies, flat boards with white spots painted onto a red background. Oval in shape, the boards pivoted on a spindle and were controlled by a chain attached to a lever inside the agent's office. With the introduction of the order board the engineer no longer had to stop the train and enter the station to receive his orders. Instead, he simply slowed the engine while the agent handed them up on the end of a long hoop.

By the 1880s the order board had largely been replaced by the semaphore. Invented by a French schoolboy during the Napoleonic wars, the semaphore soon became a universal method of long-distance signalling. The early semaphores were two-directional and "lower-quadrant." These were eventually replaced by "upper-quadrant" semaphores, which pointed either up, straight out, or at a forty-five-degree angle. Up meant "go," out meant "stop,"

The decorative waiting room at the Canadian Pacific station in Carleton Place, Ontario, photographed in 1945. No matter how they try, Canadian rail travellers can never forget the benches. With the square or curved back, the benches were, as Ken Liddell recalls in his colourful recollections of train travel *I'll Take the Train*, "the reason you saw so many people walking up and down on the platform waiting for the train." The CPR even had standard designs for benches, one with thin horizontal slats for use at smaller stations, and sturdier benches with wide vertical slats for "the better-class stations."

and the angle meant "slow." An agent put the signal into the "go" position by winding the cable round a drum with the crank. To put it into "stop" the agent had only to release a cog. If by some accident the mechanism broke, the arm would automatically fall into the "stop" position. At Lorneville Junction in Ontario the signal was located further down the track. Mysteriously, even after the signal had been put to "go," trains would grind to halt and conductors storm into the station demanding to know why the signal was on "stop." After several such incidents the mystery was solved. A stray pig was spotted rummaging in the area of the signal. The axle grease that held the signal's release cog had proven too much of a temptation; whenever the signal was on "go" the pig would stick his snout into the grease, releasing the cog and

allowing the signal to fall into "stop." This delightful anecdote is recounted by Charles Cooper in his history of the Toronto and Nipissing Railway, *Narrow Guage for Us*.

The Waiting Rooms

The thing that Canadians remember most about waiting for the train is the room where they waited. Outside the home, Canadians frequented the station waiting room more than any other room in their communities. They remember its smell, the smell of the wood stove in the winter, or the kerosene from the lamp; they remember the smell of the oil rubbed into the floor; and they remember the sounds, the silence broken only by the ticking of the station clock, and the periodic chat-

ter of the telegraph key, and, finally, the distant whistle of the train, all of which heightened the anticipation of the short-lived flurry of noise—the clanging of the engine's bell, the hissing of the air brakes, the rumble of the baggage cart over the wooden platform, and the babble of greetings and departures, then the cry of "Ahh-Board"—followed once more by the ticking clock, the telegraph key, and the silence.

Ken Liddell for one, in I'll Take the Train, laments the heavy spring-loaded doors which would slam unceremoniously on any unsuspecting passenger who didn't clear the doorway quickly enough. Also gone are the oil lamps, used before electricity arrived, which which gave off either too much smoke or too little light. Only when travellers' eyes had become accustomed to

The mail doesn't always flow smoothly; these bags were piled up at Toronto's Union Station during a mail strike in the 1920s.

the dimness would they notice if someone else was in the waiting room.

Larger stations provided separate waiting rooms for ladies and men and perhaps still a third for smokers. While waiting, passengers would glance at the bulletin board located just outside the waiting room door, where the agent would post the scheduled arrival time. The Railway Act required that the arrival and departure times be written with white chalk. Failure to do so earned the agent a five dollar fine plus demerits. In some waiting rooms passengers might read, if they hadn't already memorized them, the ubiquitous advice to "young girls travelling alone"— "Do not start for a strange city or town without a safe place to stay;" "Do not ask for or accept aid except from railway officials or Travellers' Aid;" "On arrival in a strange city,

if you are alone [and] wish the address of a reliable hotel, look for the woman wearing the Travellers' Aid badge"—or the more sternly worded prohibition against spitting.

The Mail

Another station sight familiar to Canadians was the mail cart. As the train whistle wafted from a distant crossing, the agent would wheel a cart loaded with canvas sacks bulging with the outgoing mail across the platform to the edge of the track.

Almost as soon as a railway opened its line it assumed mail service from the slower stage coaches. By 1853 the Grand Trunk Railway was carrying mail between Quebec and Sarnia, the Great Western between Niagara Falls and Windsor via Hamilton, the Canada Central between Brockville and Ottawa, and the Northern between Toronto and Collingwood.

The many gaps that remained in the evolving network continued to be filled by stagecoach and steamer. As the gaps filled in, the government in 1863 introduced travelling post offices. Now the trains could not only carry the mail, but sort it right on the train. Special mail cars were fitted up with sorting tables, destination slots, and even washing and cooking facilities. This speeded up the procedure considerably: a letter could be posted and not only delivered the same day, but (if there was frequent train service) a reply could be received as well.

In 1868 Timothy Eaton, owner of the famous Toronto department store of the same name, introduced the mail-order system. Through his catalogue, a Canadian anywhere could order an item and Eaton's would send it by train. Thus began a Canadian institution that would last over a century and would inspire countless jokes about another great rural institution, the outhouse.

If the train was approaching a flag stop with no passengers to board, the sorters would wrestle open the door and give the mail sack a hefty kick. On occasion the boot came too late, and the sack would miss the platform and end up in a heap at the bottom of a ditch.

Mail to be picked up was dangled from a hook on a wooden post, a device known as a crane. As the mail car passed the crane, a hook protruding from the mail car door snared the sack. If the mail car was not equipped with a hook, one of the clerks would lean perilously out and clutch the dangling sack as the train eased past. The clerks inside grabbed it, poured its contents onto the table, and began their sorting anew.

Many stations had post offices of their own, and here the townspeople crowded around, eager to receive the long-awaited letter from home, the *Farmers' Almanac*, or the latest Eaton's catalogue.

Wartime witnessed a tremendous crush of mail. On November 20, 1942, staff at Montreal's Windsor Station sorted mail enough to fill seventeen mail cars destined for the Atlantic ports, thirteen cars on one train alone. Each mail car could accommodate six hundred sacks of mail.

During the 1950s and 1960s the dramatic drop in passenger traffic made many of the smaller passenger lines heavily dependent upon the mail contract for revenue. But other ways of carrying the mail were being explored. The Canadian Post Office had started its first airmail service in northern Manitoba in 1927, and by 1948 began airmail delivery to anywhere in the world. Then, in 1971, the Post Office turned almost all its mail service over to the airlines. A final crushing blow, the loss of the mail turned marginal passenger lines into enormous money losers, and most were shut down. The mail had found other ways to get through, and now passengers had to do the same.

Freight

If there was a greater revenue generator to the railways than passengers and mail, it was freight. Railways moved everything that needed to be moved.

Most stations had a loading platform separate from the station itself, but from which large items could be loaded or off-loaded. Although in Canada freight sheds were usually part of the passenger station (these were

Ontario Archives S 13660

Silver awaits shipment at the beautiful station at Cobalt, Ontario during that town's heyday, ca. 1910.

Ontario Ministry of Natural Resources

Loading fruit onto a train at the Grimsby Ontario Station in the 1930s. At Grimsby, once the heart of Canada's fruit belt, the trains would creak away from the platform with seventy thousand baskets of peaches even in an average season. In 1896 fifteen hundred crates of strawberries left Jordan Station for Montreal within a two-day period. Prior to its absorption by the Grand Trunk, the Great Western Railway promised delivery of fruit from the Niagara fruit belt to Montreal or Ottawa by six o'clock the following morning.

(opposite) Biscotasing, shown here with furs ready for shipment, is a typical early CP station style.

often called "combination" stations), some communities were so busy that a separate freight building was needed. The English-style stone stations that the Grand Trunk Railway constructed along its Montreal-to-Sarnia line contained no freight facilities; these were housed in a separate wooden structure. Occasionally, especially in the U.S., freight buildings had their own office, and sometimes their own distinctive styles. In fact, some U.S. freight stations were larger and more elaborate than the passenger depots.

In early eastern Canada, the main products moved by rail were lumber and farm products. Near Allandale, Ontario, a wooden railway track linked a sawmill in the Great Pine Plains to the small station at Tioga. Horses drew the timber along the flimsy track to the station, where it was winched onto flatcars, with the longer logs requiring three cars. During timbering's heyday in the 1850s, timber trains would depart the Allandale station every ten minutes destined for the construction sites in Toronto.

In many areas specialized products dominated. Throughout Ontario and Quebec station platforms would regularly be crowded with egg crates, milk cans, salted fish, coal oil, and farm machinery. On the platforms of the northern stations freight was more likely to be stacks of beaver pelts or wagons piled high with ingots of silver.

Occasionally, freight delivery would become something of a community event. One local newspaper reported the arrival of a shipment of farm machinery at the Londesborough station in western Ontario: "A busy scene took place at the station in the delivery of some twenty-five mowing and

reaping machines from the celebrated factory of D. Maxwell of Paris.... After they were all loaded they all made a grand procession to the village hotel, where the owner provided a sumptuous repast for the entire company of about fifty people."

Some freight was live and required special treatment. Federal regulations insisted that animals be off-loaded at regular intervals for exercise, watering, and feeding. Local children often earned a dollar or so helping the agent to unload stock to keep them watered.

In December of each year, however, the freight ledgers would show a completely different array of items: pails of candies, fruitcakes and biscuits, boxes of silk, bags of oranges, and whisky by the barrel, all destined for Christmas festivities. One such barrel was spied by a group of thirsty residents of Avonlea in Saskatchewan. To avoid detection they crept along the station platform, drilled into the barrel with a brace and bit, and carried off the contents, some in containers, some in their stomachs.

Hot Off the Wire

One of the sounds most Canadians remember in their local station was the clatter of the telegraph key, for the way stations often contained the only telegraph facility in town. Initiated in 1844 along the Baltimore and Ohio Railway in the U.S., the telegraph was introduced into Canada in 1846 by the Toronto, Hamilton and Niagara Electrical Magnetic Telegraph company. The Grand Trunk Railway adopted it in 1856, and by 1860 the telegraph had eliminated the risky guesswork about where the trains were. The dispatcher

Probably the most bizarre commodity to decorate the station grounds, if only briefly, was buffalo bones. The arrival of the railways upon the prairies in the 1880's, and the settlement that followed, decimated the huge herds of buffalo. The great grasslands were strewn with millions of tons of dry and bleached bones that could be pulverized into valuable fertilizer. To cash in on this short-lived bounty, the Indians and Metis gathered up the bones and brought them to the stations, where they received five cents a ton. In the photo at right buffalo bones are being shipped by CPR freight at Moose Jaw, Saskatchewan.

at each divisional point would click out the departure of each train, and the station agent in turn would key back whenever a train passed his station.

As early as 1896, when CPR telegraphers went on strike, the company resorted to a new invention, the telephone. The experiment was short-lived, however, for the company felt that written orders reinforced the personnel hierarchy, and so they discarded the telephone for dispatching after the strike ended. In 1908 the CPR began once again to experiment with the telephone, and by the 1920s it had replaced the telegraph entirely. An agreement with Bell Telephone granted free transportation to telephone company employees in exchange for free telephone rental.

The telegraph was not only vital to the railway for train movement, but turned into a major moneymaker as well. By the end of the 1860s two telegraph companies dominated Canada, the Montreal Telegraph Company and the Dominion Telegraph Company. In 1880 the Great Northwestern Telegraph Company was created and provided links between Ontario and Manitoba. In 1882 CPR's general manager William Van Horne, recognizing potential profits, propelled the CPR into commercial telegraphy with its acquisition of Dominion.

By 1905 the Canadian Northern Railway had forged Canada's second transcontinental rail link and had established its own telegraph subsidiary. In 1915 it added to that network by acquiring the Great Northwestern, which was then bankrupt.

Weather, disasters, stock market quotations, and sports or election results reached

This rare shot shows the interior of a water tower at Boissevain, Manitoba, that also served as an office. The stem of the tank itself is visible centre-left.

into all corners of Canada by telegraph. Commercial telegraphy allowed Canadians to telegraph messages to family and send or receive money through money orders. As the railway stations often contained the only commercial telegraph office in town, they were the community's ear to the outside.

In 1918 CNo went bankrupt, and its assets, telegraph included, were absorbed by the new government railway, the Canadian National. By the 1920s Canada had two telegraph companies, CN and CP. In 1967 they finally joined forces to become the giant CNCP Telecommunications that exists to this day.

Fuelling Stops

Many of the way stations were fuelling locations. Steam locomotives needed two ingredients, water and fuel. Once the wood-burning era passed and coal became the universal fuel, coal tipples and coal storage were built at divisional stations. But the distance between the divisional points was too great for engines to travel without refuelling. To supplement the supply coal docks were placed at way stations.

But far more common at way stations were the water tanks. Because the steam locomotives so frequently needed water for their boilers, water tanks were located at every other station. To obtain access to water in larger towns and cities, the railway simply hooked onto the municipal water system. In the early days, before piped water was common, the railways erected windmills beside the tower to pump the water to tanks. With the arrival of the coal era, coal-fired pumps were placed beneath the tank, sometimes in a separate pumphouse, sometimes within the enclosed water tank itself. The pumps served two purposes. Besides keeping the tank full, in the winter the pumps also kept the water heated and moving and prevented the supply from freezing solid.

As railway expansion accelerated during the latter years of the nineteenth century and as technology changed, many early way stations lost some of their functions and were downgraded. In addition, when the CPR and the Grand Trunk took over many smaller branch lines, they replaced the smaller train units of the earlier companies with their own larger trains. By reducing the frequency of trains, they could reduce the number of operators they needed, and as a result many of the stations built to house operators were downgraded to caretaker or flag stations. Although they retained their bay windows, they became as silent as the lonely country surrounding them.

Divisional Stations

Divisional stations were the nerve centre for railway operations. Located at 100-to-120-mile intervals, these stations were where locomotives were refuelled and maintained, where rolling stock was sorted and made up into trains, and where train crews ended their shifts.

Divisional stations provided facilities for coal storage, water changing, and engine maintenance. Yardmasters oversaw the make up of trains, dispatchers alerted the agents along the line of their departure, roadmasters supervised the maintenance of the track and rights-of-way along which the trains trav-

(above) Early housing of the sort built to attract workers to divisional points on the CPR; these dwellings at Ignace, Ontario (a double section house on the left, then a single section house) were photographed August 16, 1900.

(right) Divisional station at Fort William, Ontario.

elled. On lightly used branch lines divisional facilities might be small, but on main lines they were often the reason for a town's entire existence.

Divisional points were where railway men lived. To house the men and to encourage family men to work in thesse often isolated locations, the railways provided substantial housing. For crews in transit they built bunkhouses. At smaller divisional points the crew were boarded in local hotels or boarding houses, while in larger communities the YMCA and the railway jointly constructed facilities for rest and recreation.

Even divisional stations differed in function. Many divisional points developed into huge operations. The CN division at Hornepayne in Ontario contains massive yards and buildings that cover more than one hundred acres. By contrast, Manyberries in Alberta contained little more than a small roundhouse and a watershed. Like many of the little branch line divisional stations, it existed solely to service steam locomotives. A few sidings, a coal dock, and an engine house that might contain only a single stall, huddled around the small yards. Forty-seven such smaller terminals existed within the CPR network in Alberta and Saskatchewan alone.

During steam days a train might spend an hour at a divisional station while the engine was watered, coaled, and otherwise tended to. To cater to impatient passengers, the railways instituted restaurants. Some were housed in a separate building occasionally attached to the station by a walkway, others in the station themselves. These early structures were at first simple two-storey barn-like struc-

(left) Orangeville Station restaurant.

(below) Restaurant, station at Smiths Falls, Ontario.

tures that contained sleeping quarters for the crew as well. Replacement stations contained lunch counters right in the building itself, and the separate restaurant building disappeared from the station landscape.

At the divisional point of Fort Frances, Ontario, the Canadian Northern's original turreted wooden station was moved a few yards away and became a restaurant when the railway replaced it with a larger brick station.

In smaller communities the railways would contract out the lunch service to a local hotel or cafe. The Grand Trunk station at Kingston went further; according to an advertisement it offered this added feature: "Passengers going east or west by the night trains may avoid much unpleasant inconvenience arising from being disturbed at unreasonable hours by driving to the railway station early

in the evening where they can obtain comfortable bedrooms and an undisturbed sleep till the hour of departure for the train."

Then, as snack bar service was introduced right in the coaches, providing the long-awaited inexpensive alternative to the dining cars, and as diesel replaced steam and eliminated the need for lengthy stops at divisional points, lunch rooms were closed and the space was converted to offices for divisional staff.

At Cartier, Ontario, the large wooden CPR station contained the restaurant right in the building, a restaurant that is now the roadmaster's office. At Orangeville, the separate restaurant building was converted to crew quarters and lately became the Orangeville station when the original structure was relocated to a park. But far to the north, in

CP Corporate Archives 25655

21

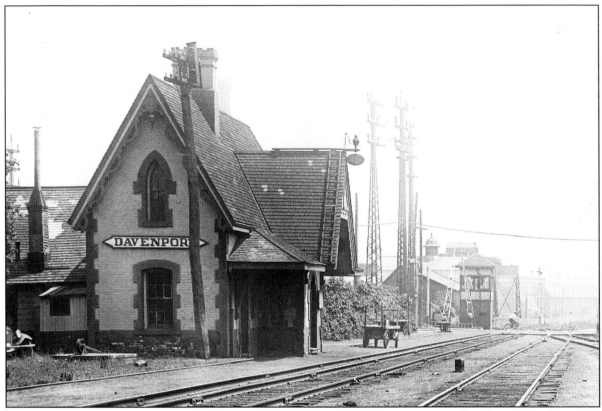

City of Toronto Archives Salmon 1057A

One of Toronto's many stations was this delightful structure at Davenport.

Cochrane, Ontario, the much-altered CN/ONR station yet contains the traditional lunch counter, still popular with local residents and with passengers awaiting the departure of the ONR's Polar Bear Express or Little Bear to Moosonee.

Next upon the pyramid were the regional headquarters. More wide ranging in function than divisional stations, these housed the railway bureaucracy. To administer the complicated business of running a railway, they divided the country into regions, each with its own headquarters. Station plans were often devised in the regional headquarters. Here too executives huddled in panelled boardrooms while department heads tallied statistics for the year.

While stations were usually part of the headquarters building, they were secondary at best. The CPR's Windsor Station in Montreal (actually, the national head office), the Algoma Central's Bruce Street in Sault Ste Marie, and the Newfoundland Railway's St. John's terminal are all examples of station/headquarters. By contrast, the hand-some limestone head office of the Ontario Northland Railway in North Bay never contained a station: the railway shared a station with the CNR elsewhere in town.

Special Stations

The recent success of Ontario's GO commuter system and Montreal's SCTUM are really nothing new. More prevalent in the United States, where urban sprawl had despoiled the landscape even in the 1860s, commuter stations began to appear in Canada towards the end of the nineteenth century. In Fredericton, New Brunswick, workers would cluster in the pre-dawn at the Queen Street Station to board the train that would take them to the mills at Marysville. At 8:30 the same train would return to Fredericton filled with restless students bound for the high school.

During the 1880s and 1890s, when Montreal was becoming a booming port, commuter lines radiated out from the city north to suburbs like Mount Royal and Roxboro and west to places like Westmount, Beaconsfield, Valois, and Point Claire.

As around Montreal, a number of Toronto's main-line stations served double duty as commuter stations. Those at Main Street (known as York), Riverdale, St. Clair, Sunnyside, Davenport, two at West Toronto, and two at Parkdale all served this function. Of these only two, CN St. Clair and CN West Toronto, survive.

As for parts west, a brief commuter service on Vancouver Island shuttled the wealthy lakeside residents of Shawnigan Lake into Victoria to work. The service was dropped in 1907.

(left) Moore Park station, Toronto, in the 1920s. Suburban lines were initially less successful around Toronto than they were in the Montreal area; one was a failure from nearly the day it opened. In 1888 a group of Toronto land speculators anxious to encourage a housing boom around the city built the Toronto Belt Line Railway. Large, even elaborate stations were built at Moore Park and Lambton Mills, while smaller structures appeared in Forest Hills beside Bathurst St., at Fairbanks beside Dufferin St., at Lambton Mills near Scarlet Road, and at Rosedale in the Don Valley. Rather than radiate from the core of the city, the line ignored commuting patterns and encircled it. Within two years it failed and was leased to the Grand Trunk for freight operations. Short sections continued to be used as CN freight stubs until the 1970s. Of the six stations none have survived and photographs survive of only three — Moore Park, Lambton Mills, and Davenport (Bathurst St.). Moore Park was demolished following the First World War, Rosedale burned at about the same time, and Lambton Mills stood as a residence until the 1960s.

Although fewer in number than commuter stations, another form of special station was the industrial station. These were never intended to be passenger stations, nor did they offer the range of functions of the way stations. They were intended purely to control the heavy rail traffic in and out of industrial complexes.

The Clarabelle station near Sudbury is one example. Originally a way station on the Algoma Eastern Railway, it became an industrial station when the CPR acquired that line, stubbed it, and turned it into an industrial spur to serve the huge nickel smelters. Because of the enormous flow of traffic, the station became one of the busiest in Canada. In the 1980s the old wooden structure was replaced by one of aluminum, and although the telephone book still lists it as a "station," it is now only a shelter for maintenance workers.

Some stations were added for special operational functions. Port Union, Ontario, a small lake port, sat at the base of a steep grade up which engines strained to haul long

Lacolle, Quebec, boasts a unique chateau-like station built by the Delaware and Hudson Railway as a customs point for incoming tourists. The company splurged on a style that they believed would give their passengers the flavour of old Quebec.

In the 1920s the CNR created a huge industrial and residential area in Toronto's Leaside Village. To gain access to its development, the CN obtained rights over CPR trackage and built a station in the shadow of the factories. A solid and functional brick structure, CN Leaside retained its railway function until the early 1980s; the building is now a dispatch office for a gas company. The better-known CP Leaside station was in the late 1970s and 80s the Village Station restaurant; it has now been replaced by an accounting office.

trains. To ease the operation the Grand Trunk built a station and yards to store special shunting engines that supplement the power of the regular engines. Although the overgrown yards and a few of the railway houses still stand in this partial ghost town, the station has long gone.

With the world's longest undefended border between Canada and the U.S., countless railway lines cross from one country into the other. Customs and revenue procedures must nevertheless be followed. All border crossings must therefore have facilities for customs and revenue officers, even through stations may not be needed for revenue or operational purposes. At many of the prairie crossings stations literally sit across the invisible line from each other. Across the U.S. border from North Portal, Saskatchewan, Soo Line engines throb beside the yellow station, while on the Canadian side a CP standard station houses the Canadian crews.

Possibly the widest range of uses found in what was otherwise a simple small-town station were those contained of the White Pass and Yukon Route railway station in Whitehorse, N.W.T. Built from Skagway to Whitehorse in 1900, the railway actually crossed into Canada near a place called Carcross. However, because most travellers were bound for Whitehorse, the customs offices were located there. Possibly to conveniently apprehend miscreant Americans trying to flee into the sanctity of Canada, the RCMP located their offices in the station and backed up their authority with a jail.

Toronto's first Union Station, 1856.

Toronto's second Union Station, photographed in the late 1870s soon after its construction.

Union Stations

Many Canadian remember their stations as being "union" stations. To the railway companies, union stations were as welcome as a shotgun wedding, and in some ways similar.

Fiercely independent and highly competitive, the railway companies preferred their own stations. Through the architecture or the location of their stations they were able to advertise their prominence and their independence. But high land values and the economics of train operation often produced reluctant bedfellows.

As urban Canada boomed in the 1890s, cities grew, railways arrived, and stations soon needed replacing. Skyrocketing land values, or simply the lack of downtown land, forced competing railways to pool resources and build a station that both could use.

Passenger convenience was another, though secondary, consideration. It was much easier to change trains within the same building than to retrieve luggage and endure

CN Archives 44365

Despite its classic grandeur, Montreal's Bonaventure station (shown here in the 1890s) was never a major union station.

The former union station at Jarvis, Ontario.

foul weather and traffic to reach a separate station to catch a connecting train.

Canada's first "union" station was built in Toronto in 1855. A modest board-and-batten building, it served the Grand Trunk and Great Western Railways. But it would be short-lived, for Toronto was booming. In 1858 a second station opened to replace it, and in 1872 still a third. But even then, between 1860 and 1900 passengers had to scurry between seven other downtown stations. In 1876 a large stone station with three domes replaced these seven. Despite extensive additions in 1895, extensions that obliterated its original charm, it too became obsolete.

The great Toronto fire of 1904 cleared several blocks of downtown land for redevelopment. A parcel just east of the station, which was untouched in the fire, was ideally situated for a new union station. To build the new station the GTR and the CPR formed the Toronto Terminals Railway Company. As was often the case, the two companies could agree on very little: the CPR wanted the station to be a stub station with the tracks at ground level; the GTR wanted a through station with elevated tracks, a design that would reopen Toronto's lost waterfront to its populace.

When the Board of Railway Commissioners approved the GTR plan, the CPR stalked out and built its own station, the beautiful North Toronto Station, a considerable distance north on Yonge Street and far from what was then the centre of the city.

After several years of delay the new union station was ready for use. On August 6, 1927, the Duke of Windsor, in what is probably the briefest opening ceremony for a station anywhere, spent thirteen minutes declaring the station open and then boarded a train for his ranch in Alberta.

By contrast, Montreal, Toronto's metropolitan rival, never had a union station. Like Toronto, Montreal was the hub of many railway lines. The Grand Trunk, the Quebec, Montreal and Occidental, the CPR, and the Canadian Northern all had termini in or near central Montreal, some more than one. Even as late as the 1920s, after the Canadian National Railway had absorbed the Grand Trunk and Canadian Northern railways, central Montreal could still count nine stations, four of which belonged to the CPR alone.

In downtown Montreal, Windsor Station was the stub station for CP lines west, Viger for those leading east. Following its creation in 1918, the Canadian National still maintained the former Grand Trunk Bonaventure Station and the Canadian Northern's Tunnel Station. Around the periphery of the core the CPR had stations at Westmount, Montreal West, Park Avenue, and Mile End, while the CNR stations were St. Henri and Moreau Street.

Then, in the 1930s, CN began to dig up the ground at the site of the Tunnel Station and proposed a union station for Montreal. With two solid downtown stations already in place, the CPR rejected the idea. A depression and a war intervened, and the new station remained just a hole in the ground. Following the war the Gare Centrale opened, but it accommodated only the CNR, and although it is now Montreal's main station, it never became a union station.

Vancouver's first union station was not even Canadian. In 1915 the Great Northern Railway, an American line, opened a large building to replace an earlier shack. For a number of years it shared the building with another American line, the Northern Pacific. By the 1950s passenger traffic had declined to a trickle, and the GNR moved in with the CNR in a grand station next door. Then in 1964 the GNR, to unburden itself of high land taxes, demolished the remarkable old structure.

Ottawa's first union station was not the better-known structure that stands today as a convention centre, but an earlier station built by the CPR. Designed in its trademark chateauesque style, the Broad Street building housed both the CPR and the New York Central. After the Grand Trunk opened its new neo-classical station on the site of the Canada Atlantic Railway terminal, the CPR shut its Broad Street Station and moved into that building.

Between 1890 and 1920 several Canadian cities gained handsome union stations. A CPR chateau replaced two earlier stations in Quebec City, while large "classical" union stations served Thunder Bay, Regina, Halifax, and Saint John, New Brunswick.

Size, however, had little to do with a station's becoming a union station. The delightful little wooden station at Jarvis, Ontario, hosted the Great Western "Air Line" and the Hamilton and Lake Erie Railway. The Grand Trunk station in Brockville and the Canadian Northern station in Belleville both hosted CPR trains, while the CNR station in North Bay was home base for the Ontario government's Temiskaming and Northern Ontario Railway trains.

CP Corporate Archives A-1120

A 1919 view of the CPR station at North Bay — one of two substantial stations in this northern Ontario city.

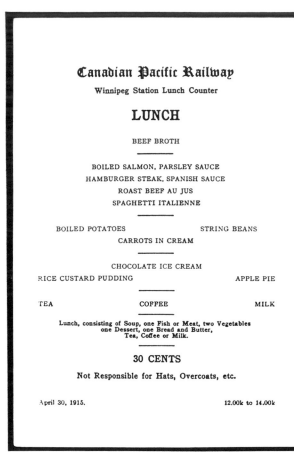

Canadian Pacific Railway

Winnipeg Station Lunch Counter

LUNCH

BEEF BROTH

BOILED SALMON, PARSLEY SAUCE
HAMBURGER STEAK, SPANISH SAUCE
ROAST BEEF AU JUS
SPAGHETTI ITALIENNE

BOILED POTATOES   STRING BEANS
CARROTS IN CREAM

CHOCOLATE ICE CREAM
RICE CUSTARD PUDDING   APPLE PIE

TEA   COFFEE   MILK

Lunch, consisting of Soup, one Fish or Meat, two Vegetables
one Dessert, one Bread and Butter,
Tea, Coffee or Milk.

30 CENTS

Not Responsible for Hats, Overcoats, etc.

April 30, 1915.   12.00k to 14.00k

CP Corporate Archives A1120

Winnipeg Station Lunch Counter menu for April 30, 1915.

The smallest "union" station in Canada, however, was that on the London and Port Stanley Railway. About the size of a large outhouse, this station never served more than one railway line at a time; it was named after the nearby village of Union.

The "Grand Centrals": Canada's Grand Urban Stations

The most specialized stations of them all, those that occupied the top of the pyramid, were the city stations, the "Grand Centrals" of Canada. Indeed, these were cities unto themselves. In them a person could buy a newspaper, have a haircut, and then relax over a seven-course meal served on china and silverware at tables covered with linen cloths. One could spend a day in them and never see a train.

The operations here were complex. With hundreds of trains huffing in and out each day, tracks had to be allocated, baggage sorted, and passengers pampered. An army of personnel, two thousand in Toronto's Union Station, bustled along corridors, platforms, and secret passageways to ensure that baggage met the right train, that parcels got to the post office, and that crew members showed up on time. It was a city that never stopped.

One of the busiest organizations inhabiting the urban stations was the Travellers Aid Society. This wonderful organization, an offspring of the YWCA and Women's Christian Temperance Union, helped the hungry and the helpless. On one occasion staff of the Travellers Aid spotted a mother with four children waiting to board a train west, carrying only a few loaves of bread to feed them.

Thanks to the network of Travellers Aid she was cared for throughout her journey. During the war they helped soften the stark cultural shock suffered by arriving British war brides, and in the years that followed they welcomed trainloads of confused immigrants. From a wartime high of one hundred thousand travellers helped, the Travellers Aid were helping fewer than five thousand less than three decades later.

Among the swirling crowds that converged from the train platforms were pickpockets and pimps. Young girls fleeing the dead-end monotony of rural Canada were particularly easy prey for the bordello runners. These confused newcomers were susceptible to a smiling face and soothing words that led only to a cruel life of sexual slavery. Pickpockets too found countless victims as strange surroundings and jostling crowds distracted arriving passengers from the light fingers that dipped into their purse or pocket. But among the crowd was another army, the railway police and security staff, alert and ready to pounce.

With as many as twelve platforms to sort and shuffle trains into, switching was no simple matter. In the sprawling yards around the stations, signal towers controlled the all-important shuffling of the right trains onto the right tracks. Although computer technology has greatly simplified the process, signal towers still puncture the skylines of the railway yards at Toronto's Union Station and in west-end Montreal.

If any Canadian station has changed very little, it is the urban station. Although trains are faster and fewer, Gare Centrale in Montreal and Union Station in Toronto remain active urban hubs, hubs with a few new

A flag station: Mt. Robson in the Rockies, late 1930s.

wrinkles. The traveller may still find a meal, a shave, and reading material while electronic voices intone train departures, but may also shop in a vast underground city of stores and then ride home on the subway, all directly from the station.

Flag Stations

If the urban terminal marked the apex of the pyramid, the flag stations were the base. Passengers travelling on lightly used branch lines or leaving quiet country areas were more likely to say their farewells from a flag station than from a busy operator station. Railway companies seldom spent money where it wasn't necessary, and areas that didn't need operators didn't get them. Because these stations lacked agents, passengers were left on their own to stop the train. To do this they waved a green and white flag at the approaching train.

Many places that started with flag stations grew large enough to earn a full operator station. The Prince Edward Island Railway initially designated forty-seven of sixty-four stations as flag stations. Within a few years public pressure and increased business were strong enough to have most of these upgraded. Conversely, many operator stations were downgraded to flag stations, the product of railway amalgamation and longer, fewer trains.

Some flag stations were little larger than outhouses: unheated cabins with a door, bench, and window. Others had small freight sheds attached and were heated by small stoves.

Although the small size left little room for architectural imagination, the dizzy days of station building and competition did produce a wide array of pleasing and occasionally

Umbrella Station, Ganonoque, Ontario.

elaborate little shelters. Some of the more un-usual, and several yet survive, are the little wooden umbrella stations of the Algoma Cen-tral Railway, so called because they consisted only of benches beneath a canopy. They were otherwise open to the elements, and were built where summer tourist traffic prevailed.

Along those passenger routes that yet wind through remote regions of Canada, northern Manitoba, the interior of B.C., and Ontario and Quebec, travellers must still stand beside the simple shelter or the founda-tion or rubble where the operator station used to stand, and flag down the train. But on the busier lines computers have replaced the little green and white flags, and alert the engineer to passenger stops ahead.

It has been easier to rescue the little flag station from demolition. Their small size made relocation costs modest, and many were hauled away behind a horse or tractor to become a storage shed on an adjacent farm. Several others ended up in local muse-ums, where Canadians can still stand and im-agine a distant whistle echoing across the forest or the waving wheat fields.

Kingston's original downtown station; it still stands today and is used as a restaurant.

A station need not be a grand edifice; many early
stations were merely boxcars. This picture shows
the interior of an early boxcar station in Alberta.

The West: A Portfolio

Mowbray, Manitoba

Banff, Alberta.

Nanaimo, British Columbia.

Taber, Alberta.

Medicine Hat, Alberta.

Unity, Saskatchewan.

Souris, Manitoba.

Gravelbourg, Saskatchewan.

Stations and the Canadian Landscape

Millett, Alberta: a typical prairie railway landscape.

C anada's most prolific town planners were the railways. The shape, the appearance, indeed the very existence of many turn-of-the-century Canadian communities was determined by the location of the railway station. During the boom years before the First World War, three national railways extended their tentacles across the largely unpopulated prairies, locating their stations and then building communities around them. In eastern Canada stations were thrust into the heart of existing communities, altering the urban fabric around them. Towns appeared, towns disappeared, towns

were changed forever, all on the whim of a station planner.

Nowhere was this more evident than in western Canada. As part of its incentive to built the railway, the CPR had received from the government 25 million acres to dispose of in whatever manner it wished. One of the most lucrative ways was to carve the land up into town lots. Each township received a station and a town.

The CPR's townsite locations were meticulously chosen and rigorously executed. Before construction began, the CPR deliberately selected a southern rather than a northern

The Port Moody, B.C., station being moved, 1945. The CPR's crew completed the move in less than seven hours and even turned a blind eye when some of the more daring townsfolk hitched a ride on the slow-moving structure.

CP Corporate Archives 12850

route for its main line: the northern would have had to pass through a number of existing settlements; the southern route was largely uninhabited and gave the CPR almost absolute control over townsite selection, design, and sales.

Although Sandford Fleming, engineer for the government's portion of the CPR, had devised a standard town plan for the prairies with streets radiating from the central railway station, the CPR designed its own standard plan. Much simpler, the railway plan consisted of a grid pattern of streets, usually on the same side of the tracks as the station. The Canadian Northern located towns on the north side of the tracks wherever possible. This oriented the station platform towards the southern winter sunshine, which not only protected passengers from the cold northern winds but also utilized the sunlight to help heat waiting rooms.

Although the routes of the railway lines were well known in advance, the locations of the townsites were not. To discourage the kind of land speculation that would drive up

prices for station grounds, the railways left townsite selection to the last possible moment. More often than not the railways avoided existing settlements and selected bald prairie for their stations and towns. Here they could control the location of the station and, rather than just avoid high land values, they would own the townsites outright and reap a bonanza from the sale of town lots.

While this strategy had the desired effect on speculators, it also caused considerable anguish among existing communities that the railways deliberately bypassed. In choosing undeveloped land at Portage la Prairie and Brandon for stations and towns, the CPR shunned the established settlement of Grand Valley, and the settlement swiftly shrank.

As the CPR began to construct its southern line through Manitoba, two busy little communities, Mountain City and Nelsonville, eagerly awaited the news that they would soon boast a new station and perhaps even become a divisional point. Nelsonville, in fact, was already incorporated and had a court-

house, land titles office, weekly newspaper, several industries, and sixty houses. But to their shock, the CPR ignored both and located its station between them at Morden. Despite pleas from even from the provincial government, the CPR was unmoved. Beaten, the merchants and residents jacked up their stores and homes and moved them to Morden. Today no trace remains of the vanished villages.

Nakina in remote northern Ontario was one of the more dramatic examples of a town that had to move. Shortly after the government of Prime Minister Wilfred Laurier completed the National Transcontinental across northern Ontario, a divisional town known as Grant was created. Here the railway built a roundhouse and repair shops, as well as homes for engineers, conductors, and crew. A short distance to the south lay another new transcontinental line, the Canadian Northern.

By 1923 the newly created Canadian National Railway, a crown corporation, owned both. One of the CNR's first fights was to obtain the lucrative silk contracts from Japan.

A divisional station: Medicine Hat, Alberta, in early days.

Success depended upon speed, speed to get the still living silk to the East Coast from the West before it started to deteriorate. But separate, the former National Transcontinental and CNo routes were too long. The CNR quickly realized that linking the two lines at their closest point just west of Grant would reduce transcontinental travelling time by four hours, enough to win the coveted silk contracts.

With the link completed in 1923, the CNR then realized that its divisional point of Grant, now east of the busiest portion of the new line, was in the wrong place. At the new junction the CNR hurriedly dumped off a box-car to serve as a station, gave it the name "Thornton Junction," and prepared to move Grant to the new site.

Soon a parade of houses and stores, balancing awkwardly on railway flatcars, began slowly to wend its way to the newly cleared townsite, now named Nakina. The townsite was a standard railway plan, a grid of streets situated north of the tracks with the main street leading straight to the station grounds.

The company houses were reconstructed along the main street, at the head of which a handsome divisional station replaced the box-car. A string of hotels and false-fronted stores lined the street behind the station and gave Nakina the appearance of the boomtown that it was.

When the CPR sought to build the Crowsnest Pass line through Fort MacLeod in southern Alberta, the Board of Railway Commissioners insisted that the railway build its station no further than five hundred yards from the town limit. The railway, however, subsequently convinced the town to shuffle its boundaries so that the station still ended up about two miles from the commercial core and, no doubt, the more expensive land.

On rare occasions the will of the people prevailed, even if it took a while. In 1945 a four-decade battle ended in victory for the Port Moody, B.C., business community when the CPR finally hoisted its two-storey station onto flatcars and moved it from its fringe location the half mile to the heart of the community. In the late 1970s the station was moved once again, this time to become a museum.

In the meantime Lieutenant Governor Edgar Dewdney had been ordered by the federal government to find a new site somewhere on the endless plains of Saskatchewan for the territorial capital. At an insignificant siding known as "Pile O' Bones" Dewdney purchased land for himself and pressed the government to place its new offices on it. Meanwhile the CPR, in keeping with its policy of avoiding private lands, chose a station location two miles away. A new town began to bloom around the CPR facility and was given the name "Regina." To further confound the hapless Dewdney, the CPR chose, to everyone's surprise, not Regina but the unlikely raw town of Moose Jaw as a new divisional point. Although Regina grew on the strength of its status as capital and the fertility of its surrounding farmlands, it never became the railway town that Dewdney and its other supporters had hoped.

The railways established their divisional stations every 100 to 120 miles. Construction

CP's station dominated the town and reflected its control over Vancouver's destiny.

booms and soaring land values inevitably followed, and existing towns and landowners vied ferociously for the coveted stations and facilities. Fort Steele, B.C., began life as an Royal North-West Mounted Police outpost. But when the CPR began building its southern main line towards the Crowsnest Pass, rumours swept the town that the CPR would select it for a divisional station. Instantly the town boomed and land values soared. But the CPR chose instead Cranbrook. The bubble burst and Fort Steele became a ghost town. It

remained derelict and forgotten until the 1960s, when the government of B.C. revived it as a tourist attraction.

Before the construction crews reached Calgary, that city was already a busy trading post. However, once again to avoid high land costs, the railway located its station three-quarters of a mile from the existing settlement. Despite howls of protest from the businessmen the CPR refused to locate its station any closer, and the unhappy merchants had little choice but to move to the station in-

stead.

The railway further solidified its Calgary location by placing its warehouses at the new site, forcing private warehouse owners to follow suit. Then, in 1912, it built the beautiful Palliser Hotel adjacent to the station, and the shape of Calgary was forever fixed.

If the CPR's choice of station location had influenced the shape of Calgary, that influence was even more pronounced in Vancouver. Under its original charter the CPR was to terminate at Port Moody. Van Horne, then

CPR general manager, found the harbour unnavigable and pushed the rails on to a tiny and dilapidated sawmill town named "Coal Harbour," where he coaxed twenty-five hundred hectares of land from the province. Here, on long wooden piers rising awkwardly from the coastal mud flats, the CPR hastily erected an unimpressive and unadorned temporary wooden station.

The next year the CPR sent in surveyor L.A. Hamilton to lay out the usual town plan with its grid street pattern. Here the CPR built its new station and added offices, freight facilities, and the first Hotel Vancouver. Until it was demolished in 1914, the grand chateauesque station that replaced the original visually dominated the main shopping street, Granville, as if to reaffirm that the railway was in control of the city's destiny.

For two decades the CPR's dominance of the West Coast remained unchallenged. Then in 1905 a new rival, the Grand Trunk Pacific Railway, proposed a brand new town for its own western terminus. On the fog-bound Pacific coast seven hundred kilometres north of Vancouver the B.C. government granted the GTP ten thousand acres of land for a station and townsite. The Boston planning firm of Brett and Hall devised a model city of curving, tree-lined streets, which the railway christened "Prince Rupert." To attract buyers the GTP widely announced that the new city would have no restrictions on the use of lots.

In 1909 the lots went on sale. Frenzied selling and reselling pushed prices beyond ten thousand dollars per lot. Despite the orgy of bidding, the new town remained largely empty. Most of the bidding had been by speculators, buyers who had never intended to even visit the place. When the port of Vancouver proved to be far superior for importing commercial goods the expected freight traffic never materialized and speculators were left with worthless land.

While the CPR located and designed its townsites across the prairies, the job of selling them fell to a private consortium of British and Canadian investors known as the Canada North West Land Company. Nominally independent, the company was in effect an extension of the CPR's land department.

The CPR was not the only railway company in the land business. They all were. The hugely lucrative land sales were the fastest way the railways could recover their enormous construction expenditures and the most convincing argument they could place before their shareholders whenever it was time to again expand.

Unlike the CPR, William MacKenzie and Donald Mann, the precocious builders of the Canadian Northern Railway, assembled their land holdings not from the government but by purchasing existing railways charters, charters which land grants as part of them. In less than ten years they could lay claim to more than 4.1 million acres of land, most of it prime prairie black soil. By 1906 the duo had created through Manitoba, Saskatchewan, and Alberta more than 132 villages.

The latecomer was the Grand Trunk Pacific. Although it was the darling of the Laurier Liberals, who built most of its line, it received no land. But by building through virgin territory the GTP was able to assemble eighty-six townsites at bargain prices. Each town plan was identical. In 1909 one newspaper headline read, "Towns made to Order."

The station in Moose Jaw, Saskatchewan, at the end of the city's main street.

St. Paul, Alberta; here as throughout the prairies grain elevators dominated the station skyline.

"We will put a town here," said the engineer in charge, "there was no ceremony, no one to applaud.... These towns-to-be would grow up straight and orderly according to a formula, the parks labelled, the marketplace determined. The main street always runs down to the railway station 80' wide and no building costing less than $1,000 can be erected upon it."

Before the town was developed, the stations presented a forlorn appearance on the bare prairies. As W.W. Withrow noted in his classic *Our Own Country* (1888), "In some places the station house is the only building in sight. At one such place a couple of tourists came out onto the platform as the train came to a stop. 'Which side is the town on anyhow?' said one to the other. 'The same side as the timber, of course,' replied the other. The point of the joke is that not a solitary tree was to be seen on either side."

By controlling the disposition of the land in the town, the railways could control its appearance. Anxious to show to the world the commercial boom that they brought to the prairies, the railways ensured that the lots most visible from the station, along the main street that led to the station and those that paralleled the track, were all sold for commercial uses. They even endeavoured to ensure that large hotels were located conveniently, just across the road from the station.

The most visible and enduring element of the prairie station landscape was the grain elevator. Prairie grain, after all, was why the railways were there in the first place. To avoid the distinctive aromatic unpleasantness of having a steady stream of horse-drawn wagons lining the towns' streets, the elevator companies located their elevators opposite the station and the town. As grain traffic increased, however, the lines of wagons grew so long that they frequently blocked the tracks and disrupted train movement. In response, the railways made land available for elevators only on the same side of the track as the town and station but at a considerable distance from the town centre.

As the towns grew wooden false-fronted stores lined the wide main street that un-

rolled from the rear door of the station's waiting room. The design was far from accidental. By dominating the main street the station would daily remind residents of the railway company's preeminence. Conversely, an arriving passenger's first view was of a commercially prosperous main street, a deliberate orchestration by railway companies to reinforce their own importance in the development and economy of Canada's towns and villages. The tactic certainly impressed W.W. Withrow: "The railway stations through the province of Manitoba gave evidence of life and energy. At many of them are two, three, or even four capacious steam elevators representing rural wheat-purchasing companies and frequently a number of mills...stations succeed each other at intervals of five or eight miles and many of them are surrounded by bright and busy towns."

In eastern Canada, station planners had to contend with already existing towns. Changes to the landscape, however, were often no less spectacular than they were upon the undeveloped prairies. Factories and warehouses appeared by the track while hotels, stores, and even flower gardens clustered behind the station. More than any other building, the railway station shaped the appearance and the destiny of eastern Canada's small towns.

Until 1853, when the Great Western constructed a new suspension bridge across the Niagara River, the village of Elgin consisted of only a handful of cabins. The instant access via the bridge brought onto the market 280 town lots ranging in price from $150 to $300. In just three years Elgin had boomed into "an enterprising, brisk and lively town

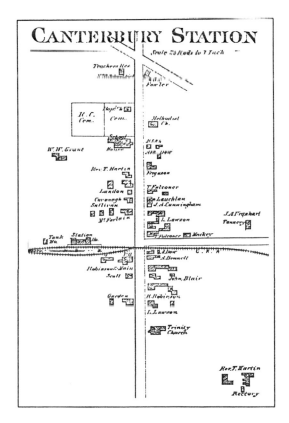

with upwards of one hundred inhabitants, fourteen or fifteen grocery stores and twenty saloons and hotels." In 1879 the original wooden station was replaced with "a large brick structure of Victorian gingerbread and ornamental woodwork [whose] massive wood parallel entrance doors made it the envy of the frontier." That little "frontier" village today goes by the name of Niagara Falls, and the station still stands.

Not far away a similar story was unfolding. In 1873, when the Buffalo and Lake Huron Railway replaced ferry service across the Niagara River with a new bridge, a town sprang up on the flat shoreline that surrounded the new station. Stores, taverns, and churches crowded the 250-lot town plot. In the words of a contemporary visitor, "Victoria, the new town, is the terminus of the Grand Trunk, the Great Western and the Canada Southern railways. It is contemplated that Victoria will become a suburb of Buffalo

[which] can be reached in a few minutes. Victoria already has good hotels, stores and neat cottages with unsurpassed facilities for all classes of manufacturing and mercantile businesses."

The town became Bridgeburg in 1894 and then amalgamated with Fort Erie. The Grand Trunk station with its conical "witch's hat" waiting room was demolished; however, another of the Fort Erie stations was relocated to a nearby museum.

A station located apart from an existing village created a new and indelible imprint upon Canada's landscape: the station village. Most were tiny satellites to the parent village and typically consisted of a hotel or two, a store, a cafe, and a handful of houses for railway employees.

A few station villages, however, boomed and completely overwhelmed the parent. Canterbury Station in New Brunswick was one. It developed around the station of the New

Brunswick and Canada Railway, a dozen miles from the original settlement on the St. John River. Within a decade it had matched the old site in size, and then, when the water-powered industries of the decaying old town became outmoded, Canterbury Station became the more important of the two. To this day Canterbury ("Station" has been dropped from the name) looks like a station village.

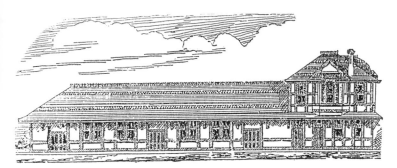

KINGSTON AND PEMBROKE RAILWAY FREIGHT SHED—SIDE VIEW.

While freight stations were seldom part of Canada's station landscape, this plan was used by the K and P for a separate freight station in Kingston, Ontario.

What is regarded as the original station still stands, a candidate for preservation under the new Federal Heritage Railway Station Protection Act. Lining the street behind are a trio of former hotels and boarding houses, while in the distance the water tank still stands. Sadly, the station is boarded up, the water tank overgrown, and the rails rusty and silent.

Even more dramatic was the growth of Killaloe Station on the Ottawa, Arnprior and Parry Sound Railway in Ontario. As early as the 1840s and 1850s, Killaloe was a small but busy mill village. John Booth and his railway builders, however, chose a route two miles north, and the station village quickly outgrew the old mill village. Today Killaloe Station is simply called Killaloe and claims a population of just over six hundred. The older village has shrunk to a tiny clutch of homes huddled around the old general store and mill.

But the impact of the railway station upon the urban landscape can just as easily be overstated. For often there was none. Along branch lines with little activity, stations were mere flag stops. Structures were little more than shelters, enclosed, and, if the passengers were fortunate, equipped with a stove. Usually, however, they were unheated and about the size of an outhouse. Here the station remained alone on the landscape, often a solitary silhouette against an open sky.

Some people, it seems, were never happy, not with the station location, the condition, or the name. The Board of Railway Commissioners, set up in 1903 to oversee station problems, heard them all.

Shortly after the Atlantic Quebec and Western Railway was completed up to the Gaspé Peninsula in 1912, the residents of Percé began to complain to general manager J.S. Gordon. The nearest agent, they complained, was at Cape Cove, eight miles away, and he refused to check baggage through Percé. Prepaid express was often delayed a day. Gordon replied that the revenue at Perce could never cover and agent's salary. The Board of Railway Commissioners heard the case and compromised by ordering a summer agent at Percé.

Residents of a locality known as Ashmont, Alberta, were outraged that the CNR would grant that name to a station located eight miles away. They argued that it was an affront to the Canadians who died during World War I. "They resent the placing of this name in a foreign settlement," read the report of the Board of Railway Commissioners looking into the complaint. The "foreign" element in the CNR's Ashmont consisted of a single Russian store. The complaint was rejected.

The residents of St. Paul L'Ermite, on the Canadian Northern Quebec Railway, complained bitterly about their station in 1903. It was not clean, they complained. It offered no heat or light and could only accommodate twelve passengers. The railway had provided nothing more than a freight car for a freight shed, and the freight platform was narrow and often overloaded with merchandise. The Board of Railway Commissioners agreed and ordered the building of a proper freight shed.

The Board was constantly checking that railways kept their stations in good order. "There are quite a few of the stations in this system [the Quebec Montreal and Southern] which are altogether inadequate for the requirements of the road," lamented a Board inspector in 1908. "I am informed, however, that they are busy getting out plans and estimates for new stations at the most important points.

Despite the different shapes that the railways created in towns east and west, the landscapes that immediately surrounded the station were similar. They had to be.

Part and parcel of Canadian stations' immediate landscape were the water tanks. The steam engines' heavy appetite for water meant that a reliable supply of good quality water was essential. The tanks themselves were steel, a bulbous tank atop stocky legs and pipes. Throughout most of the country, however, frigid winters could freeze solid even an entire tankful of water. To prevent freezing, a protective wooden shell was build around the tanks. Inside the shell a stove and pump kept the water both moving and thawed during the winter.

At some eastern Ontario stations the lower section of the shell was of local stone rather than wood.

A rod that pierced the roof of the tank rested on a floating ball and alerted maintenance crews to the level of the water inside. In the early days of Canada's stations, before municipal water pipes were constructed and extended to the station grounds, wind mills beside the tanks pumped the water from a well into the tank.

In the early days, coal was loaded from the coal pile onto the coal tenders by a bucket or scoop on the end of a swivel. This awkward process was replaced by the coal dock or tipple. With this much more efficient system, the coal was stored in an overhead bin, and when the tender was underneath the operator would simply open the chute and fill the tender. During the 1920s these dark and dusty towers became an integral part of the station landscape, particularly at divisional stations.

In Avonlea, Saskatchewan, foreman Jack Dalrymple tried to brighten his dusty coal dock by placing flowers in the window.

As pioneers struggled to clear the trees, the sawmill became a common sight beside most stations. The forests were quickly cleared and the sawmills closed. As farming became increasingly profitable the railways began to move farm products to market, and grain elevators, usually associated with the prairie landscape, became a common sight in Ontario and Quebec.

Stockyards too were a common element of the station's immediate landscape. Towns often vied vigorously with other for a stock yard down at the station. Even where cattle were not raised locally regulations required that while enroute to market cattle be off-loaded at regular intervals for exercise.

In divisional towns the landscape around the station was heavily dominated by railway structures. Sidings, roundhouses, engine sheds, and coal tipples dominated the railway yards around the divisional stations. Behind the station, bunkhouses, hotels, or occasionally YMCAs would house train crews awaiting their return shift.

Divisional towns were home to the railway crews. To attract good workers, preferably family men, the railways provided permanent housing. Styles were often reminiscent of the station themselves. But in all cases the houses could be readily distinguished by their rigid rows and identical designs.

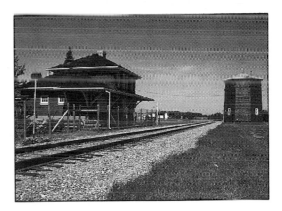

Glaslyn, Saskatchewan, has preserved its water tank and its station, a true prairie station landscape.

The original dining hall at the divisional station at Broadview Saskatchewan, ca. 1890s. Beside the station, and sometimes in it, a restaurant provided meals for passengers waiting for the engines to be serviced and the crews to change shifts. Usually the restaurants were franchised out to private operators, but some were operated by the railways themselves. At any event, they provided economy-minded travellers with a less expensive alternative to the dining car.

Gardens

One of the most distinctive features of Canada's station landscape, and one of the least remembered, was the station gardens. Early stations, with their piles of cordwood and muddy grounds, were criticized for their unkempt appearance. To soften the unsightliness the railways began to supply agents with flowers to add to their own vegetable gardens.

Long a practice of station agents in England, the station gardens first appeared in Canada along the Grand Trunk Railway between Toronto and Montreal and along the Ontario Simcoe and Huron (later the North-ern) Railway between Toronto and Collingwood. The man who started it all was Fred Cumberland. An engineer hired from England by the OS and H, Cumberland was meticulous in the running of his railways and insisted that his railway have the best station gardens.

Bolstered by the unexpected popularity of the gardens, Cumberland hired a gardener at Couchiching Point to set up a permanent greenhouse.

In 1868 two of the more popular station gardens, those at Sunnidale and Stayner, cost $436 and $401 respectively. Collingwood and Allandale, however, were the most important points on the line, and Cumberland gave them the best gardens. Within two decades of

the opening of the railway, Collingwood had become an important tourist destination: passengers disembarked here to transfer to Georgian Bay steamers. While awaiting their connections they admired the large gardens or listened to the music from its bandshell.

If the Northern Railway was the first to establish station gardens, the CPR was the most ambitious. Like the Northern, the CPR had an economic motive for its gardens. One of western Canada's preeminent developers, the CPR wanted to attract settlers. Promotional literature that featured a photo of a lush station garden made an otherwise arid Canadian West look more fertile than was usually the case. As David Hysop, a real estate agent and claims adjuster for the railway, urged, "If you want to show how good the soil is, why not have gardens at the railway stations in which flowers and vegetables can be grown?"

For his initiative Hysop was promptly put in charge of forty-four gardens between Brandon and Golden. Even the surly and cynical CPR president William Van Horne caught the garden fever and correlated gardening with virtue: "the station agent with a nice garden," he declared, "is the agent who has a clean station, has a flower in his buttonhole, wears his coat, and has well-brushed boots."

Although hugely unpopular for its monopolistic practices and its community insensitivity, the CPR gained many supporters for its gardens. Magazines such as the *Canadian Horticulturist* and the *Canadian Municipal Journal* praised the CPR for its work on station beautification. "The man who has a nice garden," swooned the *Municipal Journal*, "is not the man who spends his time in the nearest saloon, nor the man who has to be discharged

The garden outside the CP station at Peterborough, Ontario, as it was in earlier years. The station is the oldest surviving CP station in Ontario.

Staff stand in front of the Grand Trunk's Allandale station (now Barrie, Ontario). The Allandale garden was particularly large and attractive, and became so important to the community that years later the employees of the railway erected in it a bust to honour Fred Cumberland, the man who insisted upon beauty. Although the fountain and flowers have gone, the bust of Cumberland still gazes soberly from what is now a neatly trimmed parkette.

for beating his wife. [He is] a decent industrious man who will bring up his children to be the best kind of citizens."

Station gardens were often the town's only parkland and became the focus of the community. Those at Red Deer and Fort McLeod boasted a circular arrangement dominated by a bandshell or a fountain. Broadview, Regina, and Kenora also contained magnificent station gardens. By contrast, simpler gardens might only have the town name spelled out in whitewashed boulders.

To encourage agents to plant gardens the railways set up nurseries, usually under the auspices of a Forestry Department. Those of the CPR were in Wolseley (Saskatchewan), Springfield (Manitoba), Fort William, Kenora, Winnipeg, Moose Jaw, Calgary, Revelstoke, and Vancouver. The Forestry Department also oversaw the design and planting of the station grounds themselves. They established design criteria, circulated catalogues, and subjected the gardens to formal inspection. They also initiated a competition, awarding fifty dollars to the best garden in each district or division.

World War I brought with it a temporary lull in the CPR's garden-beautiful program. Harkening to the federal government's plea for more domestic food production, the CPR ploughed under many of the flower beds and replaced them with less attractive but more essential potatoes.

The end of the war brought more gardens, but also more bureaucracy. The CPR's main competitors, the CNo and the GTP, had just completed their transcontinental lines when the war broke out. The crippling financial restrictions of the war drove both into bankruptcy, and the Canadian government set up the Canadian National Railway to assume operation of these and other bankrupt lines. Anxious to capture some of the CPR's business, the new CNR also set up a Forestry Department and launched a garden program.

In an effort to stay ahead of the CNR and modernize its gardens, the CPR established a floral committee and encouraged agents to replace the earlier, more formal gardens with those more current in concept. The tradition-

About the time this view was taken of the Red Deer, Alberta, station and garden in 1920, the CPR was trying to move away from its more formal straight line gardens into freer flowing designs. Most agents ignored the trend.

minded agents, however, largely ignored the new styles and kept to their familiar gardens, formal and usually fenced.

If the end of the First World War fostered station gardens, the end of the Second World War finished them. As cars replaced the passenger train and modern technology reduced the community's reliance upon its stations, the public paid less and less attention to the gardens.

Flower beds were replaced by lawns, surrounded by hardy and protective carragana hedges. Then, in response to the greater demand for parking, the lawns were paved with asphalt. Finally, the stations themselves were demolished by the thousands, to be replaced by junkyards, modern office towers, or nothing. In other towns small parks mark the former station gardens, many dominated by war memorials. Meanwhile, among the ghost towns of the prairies the only evidence that there was ever a garden or even a station are the overgrown lawns and the unkempt yet distinctive carragana hedges.

Hotels

It was not just railway gardens and structures that typified the station landscape. Almost as inevitable as the flowers and towers were the station hotels. Every town had one, and sometimes more. Large, small, brick, stone, or wood, they could be found across the street behind the station.

In the smaller communities the hotels were typically wood and were two, or at most three, storeys high. Larger communities might warrant a hotel made of brick, perhaps with an elevator. Divisional towns could count on a string of hotels, for here travellers often overnighted while awaiting their connecting train.

In the larger cities the railways themselves built large hotels, some of the most beautiful in the country. The Palliser Hotel in Calgary, the Royal Alexandra in Winnipeg (demolished), and the Hotel Vancouver were all built by the CPR. The Fort Garry in Winnipeg, the Royal York in Toronto, the Chateau Laurier in Ottawa, and the Bessborough Hotel in Saskatoon are other examples of railway hotels that have achieved architectural acclaim.

The "chateau" period of station architecture greatly influenced many of these hotels, such as the Fort Garry, the Chateau Laurier, and the Bessborough. In a few cases, such as MacAdam, Medicine Hat, and the second Moose Jaw station, all chateauesque, the railways built the hotels right in the stations themselves.

In an era when all travel was by train, hotels were essential. Travelling salesmen, entertainers, indeed any visitor, relied upon this form of accommodation. "Drummers," as the salesmen were called, often used their hotel rooms to display to prospective purchasers their latest line of wares and encourage clients with gifts of cigars or whiskey.

With the elimination of passenger service along most lines, the hotels were either demolished or converted to other uses: apartments, taverns, stores. In the ghost towns of Alberta and Saskatchewan many sit empty, paint peeling, shutters banging in the prairie wind.

At least one former railway hotel was featured in a Canadian television show. The Buffalo Café in Red Deer, Alberta, provided the backdrop for a k. d. lang special, "Buffalo Café."

Names

Less visible, but equally significant, was the influence that stations had upon community names. In eastern Canada, where the railway lines often passed near existing towns and villages, the railway companies usually bestowed upon the station the same name as the town. Where the railway created a separate satellite settlement, the company simply

In Perth-Andover, New Brunswick a pair of hotels stare at the station.

added the word "station" to the town name. The result has been that in eastern Canada more than two hundred such communities contain "station" in their names.

But in western Canada the railways created the communities, and exercised a free and often imaginative hand in the naming of their stations. Originally, stations were simply numbered, but as soon as a post office was proposed a proper name became necessary. Although it was the practice of all railway companies to name stations after their more prominent officials, some went further. During the World War I employees who had been decorated for their war service were rewarded by having a station named for them. Heskith, Kirkpatrick, Thrasher, and Unwin were all named after decorated railway officials.

The Grand Trunk Pacific named eighty-six new communities alphabetically from east to west, for example; Atwater to Zelona and Allan to Zunbro. Acronyms too were popular. For example, Canora, Saskatchewan, was named for the *CA*nadian *NO*rthern *RA*ilway, and Kenora, Ontario, was named after *KE*ewatin (a nearby town), *NO*rman (the first postmaster), and *RA*t Portage, the community's first name. Near the Alberta–Saskatchewan border the rationale for the acronym "Alsask" is self evident; not so for the next station on the line, "Mantario." Apparently the company wished to offend no one.

Humour occasionally influenced the naming of stations. To avoid duplication the letters of a name were either reversed or rearranged. For example, "Leonard" became the CPR's "Draneol," Ontario, and "Sullivan" became "Vinsulla."

Not all station names were universally accepted. When the Algoma Central Railway decided to use the Indian names "Ogidaki," "Mashkode," and "Mekatina" for three of their stations north of Sault Ste Marie, the *Sault Star* derisively remarked that the names

In northern Ontario the CPR named its station at Bonheur after turn-of-the-century French feminist Rosa Bonheur, an artist who wore trousers and smoked cigars. Her significance to the CPR remains a mystery to this day.

were "devised by a Welshman who talks Russian with the Aberdeen inflection." It added xenophobically that the names were "designed to keep the coming Scandinavians at home." Nevertheless, the names were retained and remain in use.

***

The landscapes created by the stations are vastly changed now. The wholesale station demolition of the 1960s and 1970s left a hideous hole in the heart of small town Canada. In place of the sturdy stations and their gardens are vacant and weedy grounds, dusty parking lots, or unkempt storage yards. The water towers and the coal tipples are gone, as are most of the cattle yards and many of the grain elevators. The railway houses have been resold, re-sided, and remodelled, although the characteristic rows and shapes remain unmistakable. The satellite station settlements at the fringes of the larger towns have now been swallowed by faceless urban sprawl. On the prairies the wide main streets that ended at the station are still lined with simple store fronts and still end at the railway track. But the vacant view down those streets now seems strangely empty, for the heart of the community is gone. Sometimes only the name survives.

"Miserable Shanties":
Canada's First Stations

66 Arrived in St. Johns for a cold collation in the Rail Station house, which was pleasantly cool and decorated with green branches." The date was July 21, 1836, and the occasion was the opening of Canada's first railway station, the St. John sur Richelieu terminus of the Champlain and St. Lawrence Railway.

Built as a portage railway to shuttle freight and passengers from steamers plying the St. Lawrence to those on the Richelieu, the C and L had only a pair of primitive stations at its termini of Laprairie and St. John. According to an 1835 report by the railway's chief engineer, William R. Casey, these stations were barnlike in appearance, measured "ten feet by forty feet...[and were] substantially built and intended to be finished without unnecessary expense."

Before that, Canada's railways had no stations. The first rail operations were simple industrial tracks. For the construction of the Fortress of Louisburg in the 1720s, horses hauled wagons filled with quarry stone over wooden rails to the construction site. During the 1820s Colonel John By used a short horse-drawn railway to drag quarry stones for the construction of the Rideau Canal at Hog's Back Falls near Bytown (to be later known as Ottawa).

In the 1830s, when the railways in England and the United States began to carry passengers, there were few provisions for their comfort. Like travellers on stagecoaches and canals, railway patrons were forced to purchase their tickets in the nearest inn and there await the train. Early train notices listed street intersections as points of departure. "Starts every morning from the corner of Broad and Race Street," read the ad for the pioneer fast line to Pittsburg in 1837.

Many consider the Baltimore and Ohio station at Mount Clare, Baltimore (now a museum) to be the first railway station in North America. Even so, this large brick building at first had no accommodation for passengers, simply a ticket booth.

Railway builders had no idea what a station should be or should look like. They were not always referred to as "stations" some travellers preferring the traditional stagecoach term of "stopping place." The Mount Clare station was designed after a tollhouse.

By the time Canada's first major railway line, the St. Lawrence and Atlantic, was completed in 1853, station builders were begin-

A classical painting by A. Sheriff Scott depicts the first station of the Montreal and Lachine Railway, built in 1847. Like many of the early North American train sheds, this one resembled a large wooden barn with a track through the middle, lit by large windows and capped by a cupola. The terminal at this end, wrote the *Montreal Witness* on the station's opening in 1847, "though not boasting of much architectural ornament, will be a very spacious and comfortable building." It was situated at the corner of Bonaventure Street and Rue St. Antoine near what would become the site of the Grand Trunk Railway's famed Bonaventure Station. The M and L was a portage railway, a seven-and-a-half-mile route that simply bypassed the Lachine rapids of the St. Lawrence River.

CN Archives

ning to pay more attention to the role of the building and the needs of passengers. The *Montreal Gazette* of 1848 described the Longeuil Station as "a large and handsome structure two hundred and thirty feet in length by sixty feet in width," which, along with the next large station in St. Hyacinthe, "contained office and waiting rooms." Architecturally, however, it was still a train shed, a track and platform under a single roof more closely resembling an engine house than the track-side station that Canadians today remember.

The first railway in what would become Ontario, the Erie and Ontario, was likewise a horse-drawn portage line built to bypass Niagara Falls. Its terminus at Queenston consisted of a primitive shed and warehouse, while

that at Chippewa was a steamboat wharf. After it was absorbed by the Canada Southern and later the Michigan Central, it was extended to both Niagara-on-the-Lake and Fort Erie. It began to promote tourism and added tourist stations at Niagara Falls, as well as several way stations at frequent intervals along its route.

After 1850 railway madness swept North America. By 1870 over 70 railway charters had been approved. Not all, of course, were fulfilled. One of the first problems to resolve was where to put the stations. Station builders had to consider the location of wood and water, the existence of towns or villages, the willingness of landowners to sell at reasonable prices, and obstacles like hills and valleys.

Prince Edward Island Public Archives 3563/1

Railways would not locate a station on either a hill or a curve. On the upgrade it would have proved almost impossible for a larger train to start, on the downgrade almost impossible to stop. Furthermore, steam engines required a half mile of level track to the foot of a grade to allow for acceleration. A grade steeper than fifteen feet per mile was considered unsafe for an approach to a station. Curves were avoided to give approaching engineers ample opportunity to view any unexpected traffic sitting at a station.

Another basic requirement was water. The quantities of water needed to power the huge black boilers were so enormous that a steam engine could exhaust its reserve of water in just twenty-five miles.

But perhaps the most important consideration was the location of present or future paying customers. The railways were in the business of making money. And to make that money, especially when railways began to compete with each other, its well-heeled industrial customers had to be pampered. Proximity was the key.

When railways passed through existing towns and cities, stations were located as close as possible to factories and stores. Passengers didn't generate as much revenue as freight and were accordingly relegated to secondary status. It was easier and cheaper to make the passengers come to the train than to take the railway to them.

In Quebec many of the little country villages sat close together, located on the many twisting wagon roads that wound across the countryside. To best obtain access to these customers, the railways had to locate their stations much closer together than railway operations actually required.

On the unpopulated prairies, the stations preceded the towns. Locations there were determined not by existing clients but by anticipated ones. Elevators and stations were therefore located at six- to eight-mile intervals, the farthest that a farmer could urge his horses over rutted prairie trails in a single day to bring his wheat to a railside grain elevator. Another player in station location was the Board of Railway Commissioners. Created in 1903 under the new Railway Act, the board could dictate not only a station's location but also its plan.

One intangible factor in station location

stood out above all others: local lobbying. From the many towns that a railway proposed to pass through or near, politicians, businessmen, and landowners, all eager to realize a political or financial windfall from a station location, tried to outbid, outboast, or outbribe their competitors. The CPR's blustery president, William van Horne, took full advantage of incentives and claimed that his company would "locate the station where we receive the most liberal treatment."

One example of local influence upon a station location is recounted in the Belden Atlas of Kent County, Ontario. Here, near the city of Chatham, a family called Thompson owned a large parcel of land that lay in the path of the Great Western rail line. The family offered the company a free parcel of land if the GWR would locate the station upon it. With the station in place, the family were then able to carve up the rest of their land into residential and commercial lots and offer these for sale, creating a town plot that quickly boomed to a population of 600 and that would go on to become the town of Newbury.

Sometimes the strategy would backfire. To attract a station on the Hamilton and Northwestern Railway to the town of Beeton, Ontario, a local landowner offered free land and the town offered free water. Unfortunately for Beeton residents, whenever an engine began to take on water, a frequent occurrence on the busy line, all the taps in town would go dry.

In Barry's Bay, Ontario, landowner Frank Strafford offered the Ottawa, Arnprior and Parry Sound Railway, the logging railway of lumber baron John Rudolphus Booth, free land for a station; he then waited for the ex-

pected windfall. According to Neil MacKay in his authoritative history of the OAPS, "Over the Hills to Georgian Bay," the railway accepted his offer but, to his horror, built the station and water tower literally at his back door. An infuriated Stafford demanded compensation. In lieu of cash the railway offered Stafford free water from its supply. But Stafford was to learn, to his dismay, that the frequent requirements of the OAPS engines left him without water most of the time. Both station and tower stand in Barry's Bay, although the line has long been lifted.

Conflicts that arose over station location were frequent and furious. In 1883 the CPR needed land along the waterfront at Port Arthur. The owners, the McVicars, would agree only if the CPR located its station on a different property several blocks from the town's commercial heart. Merchants and politicians, anxious for a downtown station, raged at the CPR, but to no avail. Only when a new station was built, more than twenty years later, was it located in the centre of the city.

Upon occasion, when a railway refused to place a station in a town that demanded one, the people would do it themselves. In 1866 Petrolia, Ontario, was at the heart of North America's first great oil boom. Located five miles from the Great Western Railway line, it lobbied hard for a spur line and a station. The company refused, insisting that the boom would be short-lived and the line would prove a financially poor proposition. Undeterred, the town, rich from its oil revenues, proceeded to build its own spur line. So successful was the little line that a grateful and eager GWR quickly took it over.

The railways did not always attempt to locate in or even near the core of existing

towns. As a *Globe* reporter, referring to the location of the Grand Trunk Railway stations between Montreal and Toronto, wrote in 1856, "In no cases do the [stations] approach closely to the villages and in some, the distance is so great as to be a serious injury to the villages as well as to the railway." But the Grand Trunk had other things in mind—to build a railway quickly and economically. The original pre-railway villages of newly settled eastern Ontario were ports; at any small rivermouth large enough to float a schooner a village grew. Those with larger harbours deep enough to accommodate steamers boomed into the towns and cities that the railway set out to serve. A lakeshore route that passed through each town would have been serpentine and would have required long and costly trestles over wide rivermouths. The straightest and flattest route, where the valleys were narrower and the rivers shallower, lay inland.

Stations were isolated in another way: before the telegraph there was no communication between them. Trains operated by a timetable, and if a train was delayed there was no way an engineer could alert station agents or, more importantly, alert following trains. To prevent catastrophes, the brakemen would have to set flares ahead of and behind the stalled train. If two trains met, the one closest to the station had to back up.

Timetabling in turn was hampered by the lack of a standard time. Each town or village had its own local time, which might differ from its neighbours by anywhere from a few minutes up to half an hour. To maintain some semblance of order, train engineers were required to stop at each station and sign train orders. Station signals consisted of

This, Brampton, Ontario's original Grand Trunk station was replaced around the end of the century by a much grander structure. Ontario Archives Acc 16931-14

Collingwood's first station, a board and baten structure, was embellished with arches. When the rails first reached Collingwood (on the shores of Georgian Bay), it was little more than a clearing in the woods. Its station, however, appeared to be its grandest building, at least according to the *Northern Advance* in 1855: "[Collingwood is] an opening in the forest...about the size of an emigrant's back wood farm, littered with blackened stumps and sparingly sprinkled with hotels and charming houses, all dwarfed by the railroad's voluminous passenger depot, freight house and office."

a simple ball on a pole. The higher position meant the train could proceed; the lower meant halt.

Perhaps the most important role for early stations was that of fuelling, or "wood up." Until about 1873 wood was the fuel used to fire the early steam engines. If an engine had to haul a heavy load, or climb severe grades, the fuel supply was quickly exhausted. Whenever his tender ran dangerously low the engineer would sound four blasts on his whistle to alert the next station agent that he required wood.

Railways like the Ontario Simcoe and Huron (later called the Northern), which opened in 1853 between Toronto and Bradford, at first contracted with local suppliers to provide the wood. George Brown, founder of Toronto's *Globe* newspaper, began as a wood contractor for the Great Western Railway, supplying wood from his seven-hundred-acre woodlot at $1.75 per cord. Before the wood-burning era finally ended, his contract was said to earn fifty thousand dollars per year.

Whenever contractors' prices became inflated, the railways switched to buying directly from local farmers. The farmers would haul the logs to the sawmill nearest the station (often there was one beside it), and there have the logs cut into four- or later six-foot lengths. Cordwood piled up around the local station was a common sight on early Canadian railways, and posed a frequent fire hazard.

If the engineer miscalculated and ran short of wood before he could reach the next station, he would commandeer the train's male passengers to march into the nearest wood lot and cut enough to continue. Or,

should a farmer be foolish enough to leave a woodpile close to the track, the train crew might just help themselves. Because station agents billed the engineers directly for the wood they used, such pilfering often occurred whether the engine's wood supply was low or not.

***

The sudden appearance of stations and a whole new system of transportation had a stunning and lasting impact upon Canada's pioneer landscape. "It is an interesting thing," commented the *Globe* in 1853, "to see those stations in the middle of the forest with only a few houses in sight...a little building set down by the side of the road for the accommodation of passengers and officials...they are in such glaring contrast to the locomotive and the train which we are accustomed to associate with towns."

The presence of a wood-up station meant certain prosperity for the local economy. Suddenly pioneer Canada, used to slow and seasonal stage or canal travel, found that communities formerly several days distant now lay only hours away. Market access was revolutionized. From miles around farmers dragged their wheat and other crops to the new stations for shipment. Wagons overflowed from the station grounds onto the streets. Sheds and stables were jammed with whinnying and pawing horses, while dirty and tired farmers jostled each other in the smoky bars. waiting for the train. Suddenly the station had become the focal point of not just the town, but the entire community.

Industries, in particular sawmills and grain elevators, vied for trackside space to gain access to the trains that could now so easily carry their products to the booming urban markets. Postal delivery too was profoundly changed. "Every new station increases the business of the post office," observed the *Globe* in 1853, "for a large number of newspapers are immediately demanded in the neighbourhood and we presume that letters were in proportion."

The first stations were repetitious patterns built as quickly and cheaply as possible so that the railway could become operational and generate revenue. "American stations," lamented one cynical traveller, "are conspicuous by the absence of accommodation and convenience. They are little more than rough sheds giving shelter, while the absence of platforms and railway officials tends to mark...these stopping places."

Canada's first stations fared no better. A *Globe* reporter travelling the newly opened Great Western line between Hamilton and Windsor found that the line followed the American practice of building stations quickly and cheaply: "One feature did...disappoint us very much, and that is the station houses. They are small and shabbily fitted up in no way worthy of so great a work." "Miserable shanties!" moaned a writer for the *Toronto Colonist*, referring to some of the Grand Trunk Railway's early wooden stations.

Many communities knew only a boxcar as their first station. Following railway construction in western Canada, stations and water tanks were built at every other siding. The remaining sidings were given boxcars to function as stations until the community grew

large enough to warrant a more substantial structure. Pioneer settlers have recalled arriving in the West, a piece of paper in their hand telling their section number, and finding only a silent boxcar as a station, behind it the bare and windswept prairie where perhaps a town might grow.

The boxcars contained a tiny bedroom at one end, an office at the other, and in between a waiting room with a bench and the ever-present stove. As freight traffic increased, the railway brought in a second boxcar. Some early Canadian Northern stations were no more than tents with a telegraph key perched upon a packing case.

In their haste to get their trains running, railways often grabbed whatever was handy and converted it into a station. Across the country stores, hotels, even private homes were pressed into service as early stations. In Whitbourne, Newfoundland, the station was located in a hotel, while the Avondale station, Newfoundland's oldest, began life, according to one source, twenty years before the railway was built as a telegraph repeater station. When the Canadian Northern needed a terminal for its line into Calgary it bought a former school; the structure still stands today. If any Canadian city should have had a grand station it was Ottawa, Canada's capital. Instead railway builder John Rudolphus Booth resorted to using a former military building on the banks of the Rideau Canal for the terminus of the Canada Atlantic Railway.

Another early form of "ready-made" station was the prefab. When the CPR took over its railway from the government, it began shipping out prefabricated stations on the backs of flatcars. As wood was scarce in the prairies, the stations were precut in Winni-

The Midland Railway in Port Hope, Ontario, moved a station facility into the rear of a conveniently located main-street store. (The structure still stands.)

Original station and docks, Vancouver.

The first station at Kensington, PEI, typifies
the style found on many of the island's early
stations.

Calgary's first railway station was a boxcar
and the first of five CPR stations for that town.

Ottawa's first station.

The Temiskaming and Northern Ontario's (now the Ontario Northland) first station at Kelso (this photo ca. 1908) consisted of a pair of retired coaches.

peg, shipped, and then assembled on-site.

In one such shipment, Picton, Ontario's, first station was enroute to its grounds on the back of a flatcar. As the train neared the outskirts of the town the engineer saw, in the nick of time, that a farmer had constructed his barn on the right of way and the station was headed right for it. Brakes squealed and the station stopped just short of the barn. The disgruntled farmer, one Crandall, watched helplessly, but not quietly, as the railway workers removed enough of the barn to permit the station to pass and continue to its site in Picton.

The first stations in what became Canada's major urban centres were, like their country counterparts, wooden shelters. Toronto's first station was one such structure, built in 1853 by the Ontario, Simcoe and Huron Railway on what was then the waterfront at the corner of Front and Bay. City officials had pressed the railways to locate their terminals further east nearer Ashbridge's Bay, where smoke and noise would not pollute the residential areas. Their efforts were in vain. It was replaced a few years later by Toronto's first "union" station, it too a simple board and batten affair shared by the Great Western and Grand Trunk. The "Northern Railway," as the OS and H had become, built its new station near the foot of Berkley St. in the vicinity of the still standing Gooderham and

In St. John's, Newfoundland, the Reid Newfoundland Railway took over for its first station a stone building that had once housed the military garrison in Fort William.

Worts Distillery buildings. The Bay and Front St. area has to this day remained the site of Toronto's main station.

Montreal's first stations were not even in Montreal, but rather on the south shore of the St. Lawrence River, and were those of the Champlain and St. Lawrence; the first was at Laprairie, built in 1836. It was followed by the Longueil Station of the St. Lawrence and Atlantic. For a time the St. L and A operated a winter railway across the ice of the St. Lawrence, until a bridge was finally built.

Montreal's first downtown station was that of the Montreal and Lachine Rail Road on Chaboillez Square. It was named "Bonaventure" after an adjacent street, a name that survives to this day in Montreal's railway station lore. Later assumed by the Grand Trunk, the old "Bonaventure" station—a wooden building with a veranda on three sides—became the forelorn subject of such media description as "a dirty barn" and "a standing reproach to the city and the Company." Mercifully, it was replaced by a "new" Bonaventure station in 1886.

Vancouver's first CPR station was a rambling wooden shed supported by wooden poles and perched precariously over the tidal flats. Another early station in Vancouver was Great Northern's ramshackle wooden shed located near Pender and Columbia streets. It remained an eyesore until replaced by a large classical stone building on reclaimed tidal flats in 1915.

Few first-generation stations have survived. Built quickly and cheaply to get the railways up and running, nearly all were replaced within twenty-five years. Booming towns and growing freight and passenger traffic demanded larger stations; new technology required new layouts; and the pressure of competition and community pride persuaded the railways to build stations that were more solid and more elaborate. In 1900 Canada was entering its station heyday.

Charlottetown's first station.

King Station, Ontario, now on a museum ground, is said to be Canada's oldest station.

The Station Builders:
The Architecture of Canada's Stations

A former editor of a prominent Canadian geographic magazine once offered the insight that all stations look alike, a generalization akin to assuring an ornithologist that all birds resemble one another. On the contrary, to even an unseasoned station observer, a glance at a railway station's style will often reveal what region of Canada it was in, what railway line it was on, and even when it was built.

Once the railway companies had passed the pioneer stage and the stations had become the economic focus of the community, the companies turned their attention to the appearance of their stations. They had strong incentive to do so.

The close of the nineteenth century witnessed the end of a debilitating economic depression. Canada had suddenly become the favoured destination of land-starved British, European, and American emigrants, and railway expansion was in full swing. Business was expanding too. Even on many branch lines the original stations were quickly becoming too small. A spider's web of competing railway lines crisscrossed Ontario and southern Quebec, while no fewer than three transcontinental lines competed for the pre-

cious prairie patronage.

An attractive corporate image meant consumer confidence, and that in turn meant revenue. To attract clients the railways began a competition that would for four decades see them try to best each other in station styles. As the end of the century approached, station builders tossed aside the wooden boxes, the simple gables, and the plain rooflines, and replaced them with towers, turrets, and arches. Gables and dormers punctuated the roofs; cupolas and sporings poked skyward. Station designers, from architects to engineers, called upon foreign flavour to influence their styles as they tried to outdo each other.

The First Patterns

Among Canada's first station patterns were those of the Great Western Railway and the Ontario Simcoe and Huron. Those of the OS and H were small, distinguished by the use of arches over the windows. Simple otherwise, they were board-and-batten buildings with a wide overhang above the platform but displaying no other embellishments. A subsequent railway executive was reported to have said of the original station at Aurora that

People waiting for the train, Merritton, Ontario. The station is a typical example of the Great Western style.

"the architect who planned it and built it should be in either the asylum or the penitentiary."

Three survived a century and lasted into the 1960s and 1970s at Holland Landing, King City, and Concord. Only the former King City station survives, now located in a museum ground and billed as "Canada's Oldest Station."

The engineers and architects of the Great Western employed more patterns. The most common rural station resembled a two-storey house with steep roofs and front and end gables. The last of this style was demolished in Wyoming, Ontario, in 1988. Larger towns received brick stations, storey and a half with a small gable above the bay window. Survivors can be found in Ingersoll and Tillsonburg, Ontario. Urban stations were also drawn from the pattern book and consisted of large two-

storey brick buildings with hip gables at the end and often a gable above the bay. These were built at Hamilton, London, and Niagara Falls; only the latter survives.

A Domestic Flavour: The Early Grand Trunk Stations of Ontario and Quebec

Canada's first truly distinctive stations were those of the Grand Trunk Railway.

Early Canadian travellers scorned the cheap standards of railways operating in the United States, often reflected in the small, simple, wooden look-alike depots of the American lines. The last thing Canadians wanted was an American-style railroad, and they feared that in the Grand Trunk that was what they were getting.

Anxious to reassure a sceptical Canadian public, the Grand Trunk promised them a

"first-class English railway" and hired the firm of Peto, Brassey, Betts and Jackson to build between Montreal and Toronto a series of decidedly English-looking stations. Their prototype came from English station architect Francis Thompson, who, by using stone Romanesque arches, recreated the solidity and durability of Roman public works and thereby subliminally instilled confidence in the railway.

The buildings were usually constructed of stone, although a few used brick, and were distinguished by a row of arched windows and a door, the larger stations having up to seven arches, the smaller stations five. Most were wide enough to accommodate a pair of arched windows at each end. Other features that set them apart from other stations of the time were that they had no freight shed and no bay window.

The Grand Trunk station at Ernestown, Ontario.

The *Brockville Recorder* gushed over the sturdy little structures, praising them as being "of the most solid and substantial masonry...[that] in no way belied the promises of the company as to the character of the works along the line."

Although the string of stations were at first nearly uniform, changes were inevitable. Adoption of the telegraph meant a bay window was needed. Some were added in wood, others in brick; all, however, severely disrupted the tidy and solid appearance that the first uncluttered row of arches evoked. Even the arches themselves, which originally reached down to ground level, were partially filled in with stone to create windows.

Extra business at Kingston and Belleville brought the addition of a second floor, in both cases using a mansard roof, while extra traffic at Cornwall and Oshawa necessitated additions to the end of the structure.

Buoyed by the enthusiastic response to their stations in Ontario, the GTR station builders applied the same principle in Quebec. Anxious to soothe the anxieties of French Canadians travelling on an unabash-edly English railway, the GTR offered them a sense of comfort through a familiar style. Department of Public Works architects T.S. Scott and Pierre Gavreau looked to current Quebec domestic architecture, and built between Quebec City and Rivière du Loup a series of sturdy brick stations with distinctive ski-slope roofs. And so, by a deliberate use of familiar domestic styles, the GTR dispelled the fears of English Canadians over an American-style railway and those of French Canadians over an English railway.

Cornwall, Ontario.

So enamoured had the public become with little stone stations that when A.M. Ross, GTR's chief engineer, suggested less costly timber stations for the Sarnia extension, the outcry was so vociferous that the GTR incorporated a number of stone stations there as well. Still, there was no comparison. When the contractor Gzowski and Company had finished, Walter Shanley, chief engineer of the new line, was moved to admit that "the Grand Trunk buildings [on the original Toronto–Montreal line] are...better than anything we can show [on the western line]."

The GTR's other two original designs did indeed disappoint. One design, unusually narrow, consisted of board-and-batten construction and arched windows: no gables, no embellishments of any kind. The other was much the same but three times the width. Al-though many survived into the 1960s, nearly all have since been removed. The station originally at Durham, Ontario, was relocated outside of town to become a restaurant, while an example of the narrow style was moved from Granton to a field where it sits rotting and neglected.

A somewhat gayer design was used in Quebec. Although simple, it incorporated much wider eaves around the structure, giving a more pleasing appearance. Only one survives, at a railway museum in St. Constant, Quebec.

Most of the stone stations survived until the early 1960s, when reduced passenger travel and the advent of centralized traffic control made them redundant, and most were demolished. Those at Ernestown and St. Mary's Junction, neither in passenger service, were spared the addition of an incongru-ous telegrapher bay in the 1890s, and retain their original appearance. Others at Prescott (plaqued), Napanee, Belleville, and Port Hope, which still see passenger service, have been modified. The original GTR station at Georgetown, now a GO station, was greatly altered in 1904 with the addition of a new roof and a turret.

Between Quebec and Rivière du Loup samples of the Quebec style linger at La Pocatiere and L'Islet, while that at Montmagny was given a mansard roof when taken over by the Intercolonial Railway.

The early GTR stations were built to last. Those that survive have outlived several revolutions in station styles, changes in technology, and the decline in passenger service. They are truly Canada's oldest stations.

(above) Kaministiqua, Ontario.

(right) Spuzzum, British Columbia.

Masters of the Pattern Book: The CPR Stations

While the Grand Trunk's original stone-and-brick stations survived until most were demolished after 1960, the CPR's first stations were remarkably short-lived. In June, 1875, sod was turned in West Fort William; the building of the CPR was under way. As the private CPR syndicate began to work westward from Fort William, the Canadian government began its portion eastward from Port Moody. (The government had already completed a section from Sand Point near Ottawa to near North Bay.)

One of the CPR's first station builders was the firm of Lamay and Blair. But after building just four of their contracted eight stations, at Buda, Nordland, Linkiping, and Savanne, all in northwestern Ontario, the firm was fired for their poor work and re-

placed by Moses Cheverette, who added stations at Kaministiquia and Finmark. Most were crude log cabins and possessed no architectural embellishments whatsoever.

The first standard station plan was devised by Sandford Fleming, government engineer for the western portion. Two storeys in height, the stations were constructed of board and batten and were noted for their steep pitches and wide eaves. These were built by contractor William Onderdonk at several locations in the mountains of B.C. and by Chevrette in northwestern Ontario at places like Vermillion Bay and Kenora, where a small turret was added.

Between Sand Point and Nipigon in Ontario the government had constructed a number of simpler board-and-batten structures. Some were single storey; those requiring agent's quarters were a storey and a half. All, however, lacked the wide overhanging eaves that typified Fleming's buildings.

Prior to taking over the government-built portion of the CPR line in 1885, the CPR syndicate inspected their new stations-to-be. Of the twelve built along the Fort William-to-Winnipeg section, William Van Horne, then the CPR's vice-president, declared the six built by Lemay and Blair and Chevrette to be totally unfit for use as stations. On the western section inspectors noted that many of Onderdonk's stations were already in poor repair. Green lumber had been used and was wearing so badly that the plaster was falling away. Others used by Onderdonk's agents had been poorly maintained.

Finally, in 1884 the CPR devised a standard plan of its own. Inspired by Van Horne himself, CPR's engineering department created a simple two-storey plan with agent's quarters on the second floor and waiting room, ticket office, and baggage room on the ground floor. There were no eaves. In typical American fashion, for Van Horne was an American, the stations were to be built cheaply and quickly so that the railway could start operating and generating revenue. Plans were sent ahead to contractors, who made their way from siding to siding throwing the buildings together in assembly-line fashion.

The station style appeared at almost every new station site between Winnipeg and the Rockies and at those locations between Sand Point and Fort William where the government had not previously completed stations. The style was nicknamed the "Indian Head" or the "Van Horne" style. This style was used even in places that the railway knew would shortly become large centres and require larger stations: Regina, Moose Jaw, Medicine Hat, and Calgary all could claim "Van

Hornes" as their first stations (although, strictly speaking, Calgary's first station was a boxcar used until a "Van Horne" replaced it). The other common "first" patterns used by the CPR included a storey-and-a-half structure with a wrap-around overhang, more commonly found east of Fort William; a curious two-storey box-like building with a mansard roof, confined largely to western Canada; and a two-storey station with a front gable, used in larger centres such as Westfort (Fort William) and Strathcona (Edmonton).

The Second-Generation Stations

No sooner had the CPR finished erecting its first stations than, back in Ontario and Quebec, the Grand Trunk Railway began to embark upon its second generation of stations.

Between 1870 and 1890 the GTR threw itself into an orgy of acquisition. Across southern Ontario and Quebec the railway gobbled up a number of short lines, many of them financially troubled, a strategy that allowed the GTR to block competitive intrusions into their territory. Their main conquest came in 1882 in a merger with the Great Western Railway, and its 1,280 kilometres of track.

The Grand Trunk retained many of the Great Western's larger stations and its foremost station builder: Joseph Hobson. He became the GTR's chief engineer in 1882 and within four years, using the Gothic revival style of the Woodstock station, he had custom-designed replacements for the outdated Great Western stations in Chatham, Strathroy, Windsor, and Sarnia. These stations were distinguished by their steep roofs and prominent hip gables, on either the front

CP Corporate Archives A 17086

A "Van Horne" station: Sudbury Junction, Ontario., ca. 1900

William Notman: Indian Head, Saskatchewan, 1884. Notman was Canada's most noteworthy photographer of the 19th century. A native of Scotland, he specialized in both portraits and landscapes. His classic portrayal of the Indian Head station has often been reproduced and has prompted the use of the term 'Indian Head style' to describe this sort of two storey station that appeared almost everywhere on the CPR's western main line.

Photograph by William Notman; Notman Photographic Archives, McCord Museum of Canadian History, Montreal 1383-view

Woodstock, Ontario.

Like the stations at Haliburton and Kinmount, the Newmarket, Ontario station has been repainted in the handsome tuscan red and yellow scheme originally used by the GTR.

Dorval, Quebec.

West Toronto.

CN archives

gable, the ends, or, more likely, both. The style was also used on the GTR station at St. Hyacinthe, Quebec. An economic depression that dragged on into the nineties, however, held the GTR back from any wholesale station replacements.

In 1895, the depression over, and anxious to compete with other lines, especially the CPR, the GTR introduced a new generation of station plans. One in particular would replace former short-line stations that had deteriorated or were no longer large enough for the growing communities that surrounded them. Although only a single storey, it did posses a variety of architectural embellishments, in the wood trim and in the small decorative gable that punctuated the roof line over the bay window and over the porch (*porte-cochere*) at the end.

Limited almost exclusively to Ontario, these stations numbered in the hundreds. Several survive, although most of these have been relocated to parks or museums. Those still in place include Newmarket, Maple, and Aurora, the latter two used by Ontario's commuter GO trains, as well as former stations on site at Haliburton and Kinmount.

The GTR recognized that if it was to attract family men as agents it needed to provide agents' quarters. While in most of the larger towns the company housed its agents in separate buildings, in many smaller communities it provided quarters in the stations themselves. These stations consisted of a gangly two-storey design, usually with a gable marking the front of the roof. They were commonly found in southern Quebec and in a few places along the Toronto–Montreal line (for example, Darlington, Collins Bay, and Dorval; none survive).

Parry Sound, Ontario. The peculiar 'witch's hat' style was used by the CPR on some of its eastern divisional stations. The style incorporates a circular waiting room enveloping the entire end of the structure, with a conical roof above.

Although the GTR used a wide variety of patterns and many custom-built stations, two other patterns were almost as common as that at Aurora. One, found almost exclusively in southwestern Ontario, is clearly distinguished by an end waiting room with an octagonal, almost conical roof. Nearly ubiquitous on some southwestern lines, survivors are now few and include West Toronto, Burlington, Jarvis, and a larger version at St. Mary's. The other pattern was distinguished by the remarkable variety in the roof line. Gables were placed at different angles and different heights, and in some cases made the station appear to be all roof. This style was confined almost exclusively to the branch lines that made their way northwest of London, which have left survivors at Southampton, Hanover, and Harriston.

After the turn of the century the GTR added another replacement style. Much simpler, it had no embellishments other than the bay window and hip gables at the ends. Exterior woodwork was equally plain. Although it too was common, none survive on site, but good examples can be found near Upper Canada Village (Aultsville) and in Wanstead, neither far from the original station grounds.

Turretmania

As the nineteenth century drew to a close and competition among railways intensified, station builders added detail and decoration to draw customers. One of the most frequently encountered was a style created by the GTR. With a gable over the bay and a turret on the corner, it became the GTR's most attractive turn-of-the-century pattern. Used as their main replacement station in southern Quebec, it was built in several southwestern Ontario communities as well. Prominent among the survivors are the St. Bruno and Acton

Vale stations in Quebec, both preserved, and the double-towered stations in Grimsby, Ontario, now a restaurant with a Via waiting room, and in Whitby, relocated and now an art gallery. A twin-towered Grand Trunk station survives on site in Goderich, Ontario.

No major line was spared turretmania. One of the more unusual variations was the "witch's hat" style adopted by both the CPR and the GTR just after the turn of the century. Purely decorative, it was used by the CPR primarily at divisional points, such as Orangeville, Lindsay, and Goderich in Ontario, St. Agathe in Quebec, and Saint John, N.B. Another was added at Parry Sound, and a smaller version appeared at Eganville, Ontario. Those at Parry Sound, St. Agathe, and Goderich survive on site. This makes Goderich unusual in that both its stations were turreted and both survive on site. That at Orangeville was moved to a nearby park. The GTR added witch's hats of its own at Chesley, Ft. Erie (both demolished), and Uxbridge.

Smaller turret plans appeared almost at random throughout Ontario and Quebec, many of them from predecessor lines. Survivors from CPR lines include Streetsville and Milton, both originally Credit Valley Line stations and both relocated as houses. Another Credit Valley turret was at Guelph Junction. It, however, was replaced by a CPR standard plan shortly after takeover. Survivors from

GTR lines include those at Don (Toronto) and Craigleith (both survive).

Perhaps the most elaborately decorated of the small turret stations is that at Smithville, Ontario, on the former Toronto, Hamilton and Buffalo line southeast of Hamilton. Here an inordinate amount of detail was incorporated into the woodwork under the gables. At the time of writing, this station is under threat of demolition by the CPR.

Even the Canadian Northern digressed from its limited pattern book long enough to add turrets to its "class three" stations at Winnipeg and at Oba and Fort Frances, both in Ontario. At this writing only that at Oba survives.

It was, however, on the individually designed stations that turrets flourished. Here the railways found added incentive to embellish their stations. Some stations were ports of entry to the country or the province, locations where the railways felt that a traveller's first impression called for something extra. Stations at Georgetown, P.E.I., and Placentia, Newfoundland, were given turrets for that reason. In Quebec the Delaware and Hudson got so carried away with turrets and the perceived Quebec architectural style that they recreated a miniature "French" castle for their border station at Lacolle. In 1888 Nova Scotia Central Railway architect Vincent Griffiths added a particularly imposing turret to the Bridgewater station. Turrets were proposed for dozens of other stations all across Ontario and Quebec. Cost-cutting, however, resulted in simpler styles.

Clock towers were another symbol of railway dominance in turn-of-the-century urban Canada. Notable among surviving clock towers are those at Brantford and Guelph in On-

Plans for the station at Berlin, Ontario (now Kitchener).

National Archives of Canada NMC 99084

tario and the CPR's short-lived North Toronto Station (the building still stands as a liquor store, but as a station lasted less than two decades). Other stations lost their towers owing to deterioration or high maintenance costs. Examples of these occur at Kitchener, Collingwood, and Stratford, all in Ontario.

Distinctively Canadian, the CPR's Chateaus

The most distinctively Canadian style was introduced by the CPR and known as the "chateau" style. Ironically, it began with the 1886 arrival of an American, New York architect Bruce Price.

Inspired by CPR president Van Horne's love of Scottish baronial and French chateau

styles, Price designed stations that were distinguished by high peaked roofs, turrets, and sturdy, often octagonal bay windows. The style was used extensively in custom-designed and plan-book stations alike. Some of Price's early stations included Woodstock, London, and Galt. He was also assigned the mighty task of designing the original block of CPR's headquarters, the handsome Windsor Station in Montreal. But it was with his magnificent Place Viger in east-end Montreal, a combination station and hotel, that his chateau style gained its greatest prominence.

So wide was the acclaim for this distinctive Canadian style that the CPR incorporated it in many of its turn-of-the-century hotels, and it was adopted by other lines in Canada, notably the Canadian Northern.

CP Corporate Archives A-19703

Viger, Quebec — the masterpiece of architect Bruce Price.

Station-hotel near the U.S. border in New Brunswick.

In 1906 the CPR created the office of chief architect and, under the directorship of Harry Prindle, built the magnificent Gare du Palais in Quebec. It also survives.

The CPR added the chateau style to its station plan book with similar stations at Lethbridge, Edmonton (Strathcona), Saskatoon, Kenora, and Red Deer, all surviving, and at Kamloops and Cranbrook, both replaced. (That at Cranbrook soon proved too small. To enlarge it the CPR crew tried jacking up the top floor in order to add another storey. But the roof, balancing precariously on the jacks, began to sway and then crashed down upon the workers. Somehow no one was killed, but the CPR never again tried to use that method to enlarge a station.)

With their steep roofs and sturdy central towers, the chateau-style stations pushed Canada and the CPR in particular to the North American forefront of station architecture and inspired many imitators. Under the guidance of its own architect, Ralph Benjamin Pratt, spirited away from the CPR, the CNo constructed elegant chateau stations at Port Arthur, Saskatoon, Dauphin, and Edmonton. Only those at Port Arthur and Dauphin survive.

The CNo incorporated the chateauesque style into smaller stations at Belleville, Port Hope, and Smiths Falls on the long-abandoned Toronto–Ottawa line and in Sudbury using the Smiths Falls pattern. The two stations at Port Hope and Smiths Falls survive, while that at Belleville was subsequently transferred to the CPR and demolished. The one in Sudbury fell victim to an urban "renewal" scheme.

Then, in 1895, the federal government imposed on imported architectural plans a two per cent tariff calculated on the ultimate value of the completed building. The cost-conscious CPR immediately switched to Montreal architect Edward Maxwell, who became Canada's most prolific station designer. Adopting Price's chateau style, Maxwell created Ottawa's Broad Street Station, Vancouver's second station, and the station-hotels at Moose Jaw and Sicamous, all long gone, as well as the surviving stations at New Westminster, B.C. and the massive MacAdam

More Patterns

By the twentieth century most Canadian pioneer railway lines had been absorbed by the GTR, the CPR, or the Intercolonial Railway of the Maritimes, who had replaced the majority of the earlier, simpler stations with patterns of their own. There are, however, many areas in eastern Canada where the distinctive styles of the original lines lingered until recent times, and linger still where stations have been preserved. In the province of Quebec the former Quebec, Montreal and Occidental stations were all identical in style. They were attractive storey-and-a-half structures with oversized eaves and gables accompanied by sporings and elaborate woodwork. Divisional stations such as at Hull, Hochelaga (Montreal), and Lanorie were distinguished by their double gables. Similar styles were found on the Roberval and Saguenay line, on the Dominion Atlantic line in Nova Scotia (where the last survivor at Weymouth was demolished in the 1970s), and on the Quebec, Montreal and Western that wound its way into the Laurentians north of Montreal. A number yet linger between Montreal and Quebec, between Lachute and Hull, and on the now-abandoned Laurentian line.

A pair of patterns created by the Quebec Central were incorporated into the CPR lines in southern Quebec when the CPR acquired the line. Single-storey stations made of brick or stone were the more attractive of the two styles and featured a large gable over the bay window. The larger style, which contained agents' quarters on the full second floor, was decidedly boxy and could not claim even a peaked roof.

CP Corporate Archives A-12798

Hull, Quebec.

National Archives PA 12554

The Canadian Northern/ CP station, Belleville, Ontario.

Military in every way, the Ypres station was named after the famous World War I battle; it guards the branch line to Camp Borden, Ontario.

National Archives of Canada PA 71077

Throughout eastern Canada the Intercolonial Railway produced a vast array of station patterns, some researchers estimate more than fifty in number. Much of this remarkable variety is due to the ICR's long period of railway building and its several takeovers of local lines.

The ICR started modestly enough with a line from Halifax to Truro in 1858. In 1860 it ventured into New Brunswick, and fourteen years later into Quebec, where it absorbed a section of the Grand Trunk line. Many of Canada's oldest and most ornate stations can still be found in Nova Scotia and New Brunswick along the former Intercolonial Line.

One of the most common styles in Nova Scotia is still in evidence at Orangedale. A large two-storey style with several dormers punctuating its mansard roof, it was designed by Walter Shanley while he was working for the Halifax and Cape Breton Coal Company. It was repeated in northern Nova Scotia and across Cape Breton between 1889 and 1900. Other examples stood at Iona, Grand Narrows, River John, Scottsburn, and West Bay Road.

Another style found on the ICR's predecessor lines, particularly the European and North American, and on the Halifax and Cape Breton Railway and Coal Company, dates from the 1860s and consisted of a storey-and-a-half building with a small dormer on the second storey and a hexagonal bay window. Examples survived into the 1970s at Avondale, Merigomish, James River, and Bras D'or in Nova Scotia.

One of the many who designed Maritime stations was the prolific chief engineer of the ICR, Sandford Fleming, who also created some of the first-generation designs for the

(top left) Yarmouth, Nova Scotia: a style common on the Dominion Atlantic line.

(left) CN station, Orangedale, Nova Scotia—one of the most common styles in the province.

(above) The Maritime's oldest station—and one of the oldest in Canada—is that at Rothesay, New Brunswick. An unembellished two-storey structure, it was built by the European and North American railway in 1859 and survives on its original site as a private business. An identical structure built in 1860 at nearby Salisbury was demolished by the CNR in the 1970s.

nascent CPR. One of his distinctive Nova Scotia styles was built along the Tatamagouche line by the ICR in 1887. Constructed of brick, the structures were simpler than those of the Orangedale style, but were two storeys in height and crowned with high, narrow gables. Survivors linger at Pugwash and Tatamagouche.

Because of their status as ports of entry, Pictou and Lunenburg had special stations designed for them. Both survive. Three other distinctive and attractive stations were built at Campbellton, Chatham, and Dalhousie, N.B. That at Campbellton, similar to Pictou, was demolished for CN offices, while those at Chatham and Dalhousie have been altered almost beyond recognition for private uses.

The early patterns of railway stations in Prince Edward Island and Newfoundland reflected the distinctive domestic flavour of the Maritimes. In 1874 the Prince Edward Island Railway had just completed its line across the island and along it had placed sixty-five stations, forty-seven of which were mere flag stops, most with waiting rooms and small freight shelters under the same roof.

As business increased and public pressure for better stations mounted, many of the flag stations were upgraded and the original structures replaced with two-storey mansard-roofed buildings, a style found nowhere else in Canada. The second storey housed the agent's quarters. Once the stock of local housing increased, the railways no longer supplied quarters in the station buildings. Unfortunately, most of these were replaced by more functional stations, a single storey in height and using a style similar to that found on the former Intercolonial line in northern New Brunswick and eastern Quebec. The only recorded survivor is the original

Kensington station, relocated to become a residence when its stone successor was built.

It is this and another remarkable stone station that set the P.E.I. stations apart from others in Canada. In 1905 the residents of Kensington and Alberton, determined to demonstrate their community pride through their stations, gathered up a supply of boulders from the local fields and built a pair of stations unlike any others on the island. That at Kensington (see p. 157) survives as a national historic site, while that at Alberton is a tourist centre.

Newfoundland too boasted distinctive station buildings. Commenced in 1881, the railway was eventually completed by John Reid and was known as the Reid Newfoundland Railway. Less striking than the way stations in P.E.I., those in Newfoundland were unembellished two-storey wood-frame buildings, with a simple dormer piercing the roof line, and no eaves. The upper floor housed the agent and his family, and the lower contained the office and waiting room. Freight sheds were separate. In the larger communities, where housing was more plentiful, the railway used a single-storey structure. Perhaps the island's most attractive station is the old mansard-roofed building at Avondale (p. 160), which was in use as a station as early as 1883.

In both P.E.I. and Newfoundland the CNR in the late 1980s abandoned the lines and tore up the tracks. In both places, however, several former stations have found new private or public uses.

Ontario, like Nova Scotia, proved to be another hodge-podge of station styles. The Central Ontario Railway and the Bay of Quinte Railway lie close to each other in central On-

Pugwash, Nova Scotia: one of the two survivors of the style designed for ICR's Tatamagouche line by Sir Sandford Fleming.

The gangly CP station at Burtt's Corners NB was unusual and found only in the maritimes.

tario, and indeed cross each other. Both were constructed during the 1880s from ports on Lake Ontario to penetrate the heartland of Ontario and haul out the lumber and minerals that their builders were certain would reap enormous profits.

Both lines used a station pattern that reflected the stark simplicity of small, low-budget lines. The smallest sample of the COR style was a single-storey wooden structure distinguished only by a large eave that extended over the platform. Examples survive at Frankford, Consecon, Coe Hill, and Marmora. Only one sample of the larger station with agent's quarters survives at Bancroft (a museum), while the two-storey concrete passenger terminal still stands at Maynooth Station.

The BoQ station survival rate is even more remarkable. Between Deseronto and

Bannockburn, a nearly unbroken string of six original stations has survived on site, little altered since 1942 when the line was abandoned. Although inspired by the CPR's two-storey Van Horne style, the BoQ stations, with their hexagonal bay window that extends to the second floor, were easily distinguished from any other two-storey station in Canada. Complete with their original exterior stucco finish, their freight sheds, and their trademark narrow cement platforms, the survivors include the former stations at Queensville, Erinsville, Marlbank, Tamworth, Stoco, and Newburgh.

Southern Ontario was the only region of Canada to be strongly influenced by American station design. Southwestern Ontario sits like a wedge between southern Michigan and

upper New York state. During the 1860s and 1870s this region provided an easy short cut for American railway builders looking for connections between borders. Soon new American lines crossed the area: the Canada Southern (later the New York Central), the Toronto, Hamilton and Buffalo, and the Baltimore and Ohio, and on them were standard American "depots." Small, wooden, and punctuated by only a front gable or perhaps a small tower, these were repeated in most towns and villages, but some outstanding exceptions break the monotony. Elegant stone stations were placed in Essex and Kingsville in far southwestern Ontario, and a delightful turreted station is found in Smithville. Large, outstanding headquarters buildings stand at

The station style used at Locust Hill was one of the more common styles used by the CPR in Ontario.

Architect's conception of Toronto's Yorkville station, ca. 1883. In design a twin of CP's Peterborough station, the Yorkville station was soon to be replaced by the towered North Toronto station.

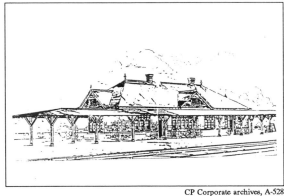

CP Corporate archives, A-528

St. Thomas and at Windsor, the former designated under Canada's new heritage stations act.

The CPR Gets Back into the Act

In 1897 the CPR produced its first new station design in fifteen years, and in less than two decades went on to produce a plan book with twenty-one different designs. After building fewer than 70 new stations between 1886 and 1896, the CPR went on a binge of station construction, adding or replacing more than 750 stations over the following eighteen years.

One of the CPR's earliest contracts was with the firm of J.W. and E.C. Hopkins of Montreal, who designed the stations east of Perth to Vaudrieul on the CPR's Ontario and Quebec Railway. West of Perth was a string of utterly uniform "Van Horne" stations identical to those that had been built on the transcontinental line a few years earlier. Broken only by the still-standing Peterborough station, this string of identical stations stretched unbroken to Toronto. Although a few were re-

placed because of fire, most survived until the 1970s. Smiths Falls, Havelock, Tweed, and Peterborough alone survive.

The CPR's most common way stations in Ontario were the storey-and-a-half 2A pattern that contained agent's quarters and the smaller "Swiss cottage" style that did not. Generally, larger brick stations were placed on the busy main line between Windsor and Montreal. Some included a decorative hip gable above the operator's bay (for example, Oshawa and Port Hope, Ontario); most others kept architectural embellishments to a minimum.

Even divisional stations were simply larger versions of a similar plan (Woodstock and Galt). Special designs were incorporated into stations at Windsor (demolished) with a turret, and at Chatham (relocated) with an interesting arch. Other early designs saw limited use. Attractive brick stations were designed for Yorkville (North Toronto), Guelph, and Peterborough, but saw no known application outside of these places. Yorkville was later replaced by the monumental North Toronto Station, Guelph was relocated, and Peterborough has been restored by the Chamber of Commerce. A Tudor revival style with prominent gables and Tudor woodwork was used at West Toronto and Trenton. Both are demolished.

Although the CPR's patterns were largely pleasing, they did create one stark and unappealing style, for the stations of the Sault Ste Marie branch in northern Ontario. These were typically long, low, and wooden, with end gables and a flat dormer barely peaking through the roof over the bay window. No effort was made to add anything to these buildings to make them in the least attractive. But whenever they needed replacing, the CPR would pull out of its pattern book something a little more elaborate. Eventually the nicest station on the line was that built at McKerrow, using a style found at several places along the Orangeville-to-Owen Sound line in southern Ontario. All, however, are demolished.

Prairie Patterns

If any part of Canada is associated with pattern-book stations it is the prairies. The railways created the towns, and the stations dominated them. Because the CPR has been there the longest, it can claim the greatest variety of station patterns. Very quickly the ubiquitous "Van Hornes" were replaced by what the CPR called its "Western Line" stations, built between 1895 and 1914. Some were mere elaborations upon the Van Horne (different-sized gables being added to the front), while others invoked an international flavour, including a "Chinese" pagoda style and a "Rheinish" gable style. The most common was what the CPR called the "A5." A simple operator station with agent's quarters upstairs, it was reproduced by the hundreds across the prairies and even along the Sudbury-to-Bolton branch of the CPR in central Ontario.

Nearly all of the CPR's more interesting stations were designed by CP architect Ralph Benjamin Pratt. Pratt, who had been responsible for widely implementing the CPR's famous chateau style in local stations, was in 1901 spirited away by the Canadian Northern railway. William MacKenzie and Donald Mann, the duo behind the CNo, wanted nothing but the best, and Pratt promised the best design in stations. Indeed, during his sojourn with the CNo he cre-

ated Canada's most distinctive and widely used station, the "class three" — a boxy, two-storey design upon which architect Ralph Benjamin Pratt placed a high, pyramidal roof. It became the prairie's most common style (cf. Gravelbourg, p. 40), and was used in Ontario, north of Toronto to Parry Sound on the James Bay Junction Railway and west of Thunder Bay. This plan even made its way to Minnesota where the CNo operated a pair of lines. So flexible was this trademark feature that it was incorporated into its divisional stations—a large divisional station of that style survived at Parry Sound until the 1930s, when it was replaced by a CN plan. Even the large stations such as those at Edmonton, Saskatoon, Dauphin, Port Arthur, and Virginia, Minnesota bore its mark. Due to Pratt's influence, the former three were nearly identical to the CPR's Broad Street Station in Ottawa. None

Virden, Manitoba, an example of the CPR's imaginative pagoda-style station. It has now been federally designated.

The oriental flavour on the Empress, Alberta CPR station, a style little used elsewhere.

A 'plan A' station; nearly two-thirds of all Grand Trunk Pacific stations were in this style.

were found on the short-lived Ottawa to Toronto line.

Prior to Pratt's arrival, the CNo had experimented with a style that incorporated a lower roofline and hip gables. The style was an attractive one, and recycled survivors appear in Gilbert Plains and Winnipegosis.

The last of the three major lines to cross the prairies was the Grand Trunk Pacific (the National Transcontinental in eastern Canada). It drew from an even smaller range of patterns than either the CPR or the CNo. Perhaps its most pleasing and distinctive was the storey-and-a-half style with a bell cast roof and an octagonal bay window that punched through the eave to become a second floor dormer. Known simply as plan "A," it was created in 1910 by the GTP's chief engineer, K.B. Kelliker, and comprised nearly two-thirds of the GTP station roster. A simpler version, more common in Ontario and Quebec, saw the octagonal window replaced with a square format. Its divisional stations were large two-storey boxes with few distinguishing features. Some interesting exceptions to this are the divisional stations yet standing at Melville, Saskatchewan, and at Sioux Lookout, Ontario, both of which feature large front gables at both ends of the second storey.

When the CNR took over the GTP and the CNo, it devised standard plans of its own. One that it borrowed from the GTP was the two-storey box, which it used to replace older CNo stations in northern Ontario, and which it enlarged and built on the Noranda branch of the CNR in northern Quebec, in a particularly massive pattern that was repeated nowhere else in Canada. CN's patterns were for the most part smaller and simpler, their single-storey style being embellished only by a gable over the bay (with survivors at Parry Sound and Owen Sound, it has indeed proved a sound pattern).

Before the Second World War changed Canada's station styles forever, the CN introduced three new patterns, largely in the Maritimes. One was a modification of Pratt's Canadian Northern pyramid but with a less exaggerated roof line. Examples of this were at Saint Quentin, N.B., Musquadabolt, N.S., and at Borden, P.E.I. The second style altered Pratt's station roof, replacing the pyramid with hip gables (a throwback, perhaps, to the very first designs tried by the CNo), with examples at Grand Falls and Plaster Rock, N.B., and St. Felicien, Quebec. The third was much less interesting and consisted of a two-storey structure with a front gable. Examples of this style were found at Londonderry, N.S., and St. Leonard, N.B. All three styles were combination stations with large freight rooms and waiting rooms for passengers.

The New Era

After the Second World War, the world entered a new era. As if rejecting the war and the debilitating depression that preceded it, Canadians cast aside the old order with all its trappings and eagerly grabbed onto anything new. Televisions, automatic household appliances, and the family car all moved from being luxuries to being necessities. With the new age came new architecture. It too cast aside the frivolities and trappings of the pre-war styles and emerged with what has been called the "international" style of architecture.

Although this style, which originated in the Bauhaus school of architecture, was

The Andrew, Alberta station is a design used commonly along the CPR's prairie branch lines and along the now abandoned Rigaud -Ottawa line in eastern Ontario.

known in Europe and the U.S. before the war started, Canadians waited until after the war before incorporating it into their stations. Characterized by expanses of glass and steel and by flat roofs, it was a total rejection of the Victorian, the classical, or the beaux arts

styles that had dominated less than a decade before. The new architecture also rejected national distinctions in favour of international uniformity.

Canada's station builders fell into line and abandoned the old styles. One of the earliest

of the new-era stations was the CN station at Midland, Ontario, a building that actually used the stone base of the earlier structure. The CPR too introduced a new-era style with single-storey stations at places like Field, B.C., Pendleton, Ontario, and St. Basile, Quebec. When a string of modern pulp mill towns was created along the north shore of Lake Superior in the early 1950s, the CPR responded with its new international station style. Flat roofed and two-storeyed (in these lonely northern communities it was still necessary to include agent's quarters), the stations were highlighted by their art deco eaves. The CPR built a string of such stations at Marathon, Red Rock, and Terrace Bay in Ontario and at Thurso and Asbestos in Quebec.

Meanwhile, in the Maritimes many of the old Intercolonial stations were nearing their hundredth birthday, and the CNR embarked

upon a replacement program. To implement the change, the engineering department in the late 1940s created a new and flexible pattern characterized by a single storey, a white finish, and a simple gable over the waiting room or bay window. Despite some variety in the massing and in the rooflines, aesthetics was cast aside in favour of utility. Then, in the 1960s and 70s, in conjunction with CN's new logo and new corporate image, the railway replaced many of their aging New Brunswick stations with a string of international style stations. Magnificent old ICR stations at Campbellton, Bathurst, Newcastle, and Moncton were removed and replaced with featureless boxes. Many were subsequently renovated by Via Rail after CN no longer required them.

Most of Canada's railway lines followed suit. The Algoma Central added the new flat-roofed styles at Wawa and Frater, and the Pa-

cific Great Eastern (later to become the British Columbia Railway) added new flat-roofed stations at Prince George, North Vancouver, and Shalalth.

Despite the spate of new styles, stations were still stations. Mail and milk cans still waited in the freight shed, passengers still paced the platforms, and the agents still cranked up the semaphores and hooped up the train orders to the engineer or the brakeman.

The 1960s brought with it the end of the traditional station and the introduction of functionally specialized stations. The most visible were the new passenger stations. More reminiscent of airports than train stations, these were almost all glass, and almost all waiting room. Gone were the bay window and the agent. In their places were glass walls and uniformed ticket agents who stood smartly behind airport-like counters. Nearly

The old and the new: the first station at Spence's Bridge, British Columbia, and that erected after the Second World War.

A Sudbury architect, the late Peter DeWit, built a traditional looking station for VIA Rail's Capreol station.

all such stations were located in suburban areas far from the cramped and congested downtowns, and to attract the car-oriented consumer, there was always ample parking.

Opened in 1967, the new Oshawa, Ontario, station was, according to CN's press releases, "a prototype of functional bright stations to serve medium-size communities." The style was created by S. Reznicek, CN's senior architect, and appeared in other places, such as Saskatoon and Kingston, Ontario.

Smaller communities were not so lucky. What the CN press releases failed to mention was that many magnificent and historic stations were being razed by the hundreds, even where passenger service still existed, and replaced with tiny glass and aluminum "bus" shelters.

When the St. Lawrence Seaway buried the original route of the Grand Trunk Railway between Cornwall and Morrisburg, the surviv-

ing stations were removed and replaced with flat-roofed International style stations along the new alignment. The station at Cornwall was demolished for a highway bridge; the one at Aultsville was relocated and survives.

In 1973, to accommodate continuing passenger service in the remote northern Ontario town of Chapleau, the CPR brought in on a string of flatcars its new structure, nine prefabricated sections, moved them by sleigh to the new site, and placed them on cement posts. A few months later the old divisional station was demolished.

Prefabricated structures became the order of the 1970s. With most station functions gone or fast going, there remained little need for anything more than a shelter for maintenance crews. Their foundations rotting, their paint peeling, and their upkeep and insurance costs growing, the old stations became impossible to justify. Through the 1970s and

1980s they were removed by the thousands and replaced with yellow prefabricated trailers, which were transported on trucks rather than rails and moved onto the old station site.

Suddenly station grounds that had once possessed an architectural treasure, a joyful focus for the community, had acquired all the ambience of a construction site. Even with their new divisional stations the new station architects turned their backs on beauty and brought large, featureless, concrete-block or, later, aluminum shacks. Two of the more hideous examples of modern divisional station styles are the CP station at Victoria, B.C., and the CN station at Jonquiere, Quebec (where the previous attractive brick station had been torn down to make room for a parking lot).

But there were some lines still in the passenger business. One was Via Rail, established as a token effort by the Canadian government to relieve CN and CP of its passen-

Canada's newest station is the ONR's ultra-modern North Bay station. The building recaptures traditional station rooflines, and features a bay window. The $4 million structure also contains a snack bar, and a display of Cree craftwork. In addition to the two trains a day, there are bus departures from eight bus bays and the station is connected by a walkway to the Northgate Square shopping mall.

ger mandate. Via realized that station design still had a role to play in attracting passengers. The revivalist era of station styles had begun: Via's architects devised three basic patterns that varied in size according to passenger numbers, but that incorporated imaginative lines, steep rooflines vaguely reminiscent of the chateau style, and stylish wooden benches.

In two cases Via designed special stations that recall the early days of station architecture: the Esquimalt and Nanaimo terminus at Victoria and the passenger station at Capreol, Ontario. The latter was designed by a Sudbury architect and includes a vaulted waiting room, a traditional roofline, and the brackets from the former wooden Canadian Northern divisional station where Via had been the sole tenant.

In British Columbia the BCR developed a new style that, although modern in its overall impact, is attractive and inviting, much like a house. An example of the style is found at Exeter. The Ontario Northland Railway, after flirting with modernism in its new station at New Liskeard, returned to revivalism with its very traditional looking new stations at Englehart and North Bay.

And so, station styles have come almost full circle. Station architects, after rejecting traditional patterns in favour of a featureless international fad have rediscovered the aesthetic values that made Canada's railway stations the pride of their community. Sadly, these are too few and far between. As long as federal transportation planners, bureuacrats, and politicians remain mired in the 1960s myth that rail passenger service is outmoded, train service will continue to dwindle and the few remaining grand old station buildings will be demolished. Much of Canada's best architecture will be gone forever, a cynical tribute indeed to the station builders.

Port Hope

Nakina

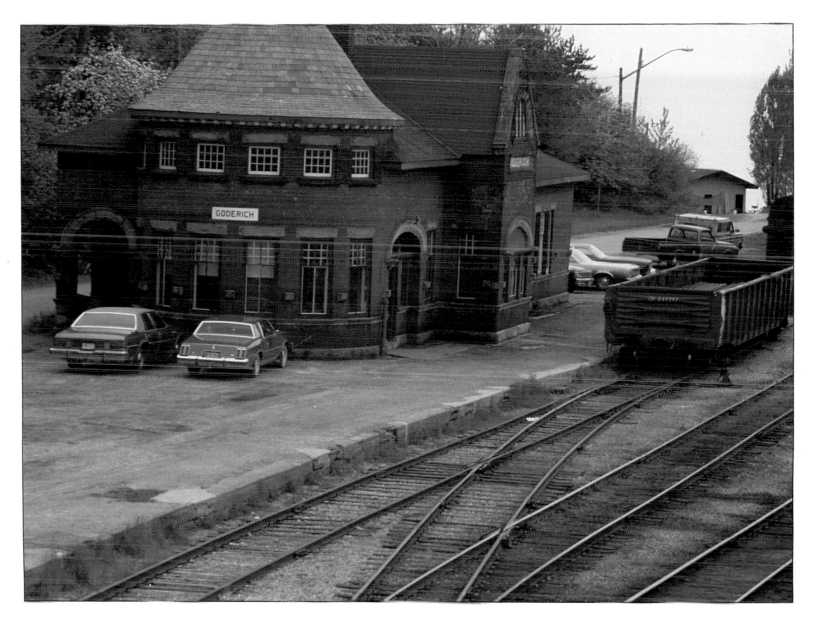

Goderich

Biscotasing

Blind River

Cobalt

Barry's Bay

Union Station, Toronto

The waiting room of the CPR's Vancouver station was one of its more distinguishing features.

Urban Monuments:
Canada's City Stations

anada's finest stations were her urban stations. In many medium-sized cities they were the most stunning structure in town. In contrast to small-town and rural stations, urban stations were special stations built for special reasons.

In some places they were the points where a number of railway lines converged. In these places simple economics dictated that railway lines build marshalling yards, headquarters, and sometimes, when that rare spirit of cooperation prevailed among rival railroads, union stations.

In other places urban stations were built just because the size of the city warranted a grand building. Inter-rail rivalry and civic pride often teamed up to force the railways to summon their best architectural talent to build a monument to their supremacy.

Other towns were important ports of entry. Here visitors or immigrants arriving in Canada would catch their first glimpse of the country, and the railways wanted that first glimpse to impress them.

Whatever the reason for building an urban "palace," the operative word was "grand," for the railways intended to dominate the townscape as they dominated the economy. In some instances that dominance was reflected in the height of the building, with high pyramidal roofs or towers; in other instances in the size of the entrance, reminiscent of triumphal Roman arches or the great pillars of the Greek temples. Whatever it was, the railways envisioned themselves as the paramount influence upon urban Canada, their stations the grand gateway to it.

One of the early influences on North American station styles was the union station in St. Louis, Missouri, designed by Theodore Link. Its high peaked roofs and its looming clock tower utterly dominated downtown St. Louis. This influence was reflected in the 1895 extension to Toronto's second union sta-

tion, in the Intercolonial station in Saint John, N.B., and in the smaller but no less appealing Grand Trunk station in Brantford, Ontario, designed by the firm of Spier and Rohns and built in 1905.

The Chicago Exposition of 1893 introduced a new wave of station styles. The invention of the steel beam had suddenly made possible the construction of massive flat-top buildings, a technique demonstrated in the exposition buildings. Steeply pitched roofs were no longer needed to create the impression of size as chateauism gave way to classicism. To the station builders the flat rooflines called for Greek columns and Roman arches and gave them a new expression for railway preeminence: the gateway. Oversized station portals replaced the looming towers and soaring peaked roofs as a means of expressing dominance. Suddenly the stations began to sport huge doric arches or classical columns that stretched five storeys high. These were the new statement, the grandest entrance to urban North America.

The third and last phase of urban station design was the office tower. Again in a par-

tial response to construction technology, corporations began to express their dominance in height rather than beauty. Called "modernism" by architects, the style consisted of soaring office towers of concrete or glass and aluminum, with the station hidden, almost as an afterthought, on the main floor or in the basement. Calgary (CP) and Edmonton and London (both CN) are examples. Nothing about the outward appearance of the building cried "station."

Embraced by urban politicians and corporate executives with skyscraper mentalities, modernism was roundly scorned by a populace that had become cynical over the depersonalized profiteering that motivated modern corporations, especially those that ran the railways. To the pubic the office towers symbolized all that was wrong with urban life, and they demanded friendlier faces on their buildings.

This wave of rejection has led to a resurgence in urban station preservation. Grand urban stations, many originally scheduled for demolition, have been preserved, with millions spent on their restoration.

Trains no longer call at the original Newfoundland Railway terminal in St. John's Newfoundland.

Windsor Station in Montreal, Union Station in Toronto, and the grand Gare du Palais in Quebec have all been preserved, rescued from modernist madness, simply because the public had had enough. Most of Canada's larger cities contain in their cityscape an urban palace that reflects one, maybe more, of these eras in Canada's station building.

St. John's

In contrast to its (near) namesake, St. John's, Newfoundland, has retained its original urban palace. Designed in the "French Second Empire" style and built by W.H. Massey, the station replaced the one-time military building that had served as the Reid Newfoundland Railway's first station.

The station builders used local stone and created arches, steep mansard rooflines, and high narrow gables. Although the trains don't run in Newfoundland any more, the station still houses the offices of Newfoundland's Terra Transport corporation and remains one of Canada's more attractive stations.

Halifax

Built by the Canadian National Railway after it took over Canada's bankrupt lines, the Halifax station falls easily into the neo-classical category. Its Greek pillars and stone walls gaze soberly over an otherwise uninteresting Halifax street.

It replaced an earlier Intercolonial station built in 1877 by Halifax builder Henry Peters and described as "the finest and most striking upon the Intercolonial Railway System." The original structure contained offices, waiting rooms, and living quarters for the agent and was heated by steam and lit by gas. This station met an unusual fate, being blown apart by the tragic Halifax explosion of 1917.

(above left) The handsome red sandstone station in Charlottetown hasn't seen a train in many years.

(left) Saint John's second station, that of the Intercolonial, was even grander than the first. The classical union station which followed it in the 1930s was demolished in the 1970s for a small glass shack.

Charlottetown

Built by the Prince Edward Island Railway in 1907, Charlottetown's two-and-a-half-storey station of local sandstone replaced a much earlier and much simpler single-track train shed. Waiting rooms, ticket offices, and newsstand were located on the first floor; offices of the road master, yardmaster, and other officials were on the second; and union meetings generally took place on the third. (It is not known whether management intended part of its corporate headquarters for the latter use.) By the early 1980s both Via and CN had moved out, and the building became a farmers' market.

Saint John

The little glass shelter that Saint John, New Brunswick, calls its station belies the legacy of magnificent stations that preceded it. In 1858 the European and North American built Saint John's first grand station, a large wooden romanesque structure. It lasted until 1884 when the Intercolonial replaced it with a stone building that, with its steep roofline and prominent tower, was reminiscent of the 1895 addition to the former Union Station in Toronto. Designed by architect J.T.C. McKean, it consisted of brick and stone and measured 114 feet by 88 feet. Three storeys high, it housed waiting rooms, offices, a dining hall, and agent's quarters on the second floor.

This in turn was replaced in 1932 by a CN station, a union station really, that incorporated the subdued classical lines that the railway was using in stations like those at Edmonton and Saskatoon.

This building lasted until 1978 when, despite efforts to save it, the CN removed and replaced it with a simple glass shelter, a monument to the railway's insensitivity to the heritage of one of Canada's oldest cities.

Quebec

Another of Canada's magnificent stations sits in the heart of Quebec; it is the Gare du Palais. Although clearly chateauesque with its turrets, arches, and steep roof, it was designed not by the masters of the chateau, Price and Maxwell, but by a later CP architect by the name of H.E. Prindle. Built in 1914 as

The CPR's Gare du Palais in Quebec City, shown here behind an ice sculpture of a train engine, boasted the CPR's chateauesque roofline.

National Archives of Canada PA 175333

a union station, it replaced an older CP station (a former Quebec Montreal and Occidental station) that stood adjacent to it, and the Grand Trunk station that stood several blocks away.

Other stations in Quebec were the National Transcontinental's "Bridge" Station, a divisional station that was built in that company's standard pattern and was replaced by the modern aluminum Ste Foy Station. Across the river sits the former Intercolonial's Levis Station, a massive two-storey building with steep rooflines. Although it was renovated by Via and the city of Levis, the tracks have been lifted and Via's passengers are now dropped off outside of the town.

The CPR's Windsor Station in Montreal. Designed by Bruce Price in 1886, the building was opened in 1889. Van Horne proudly proclaimed in six-foot letters that it "Beats All Creation, the New CPR Station." An 1897 CPR guidebook described the station as having "a rare combination of elegance, comfort and architectural beauty, undoubtedly one of the handsomest buildings in the city and a fitting illustration of the enterprise of the CPR."

Montreal

CPR's first Montreal station was anything but grand. The Dalhousie Square Station in east-end Montreal, which the CPR had inherited from the Quebec, Montreal and Occidental Railway, was a solid but simple structure, noteworthy only for its high windows and use of stone and brick.

It was soon superseded by Bruce Price's chateauesque Viger Station and hotel, built in 1896. Price's use of high peaked roofs, dormers, gables, and turrets made and continue to make the Viger Station one of Montreal's more elegant buildings. When the Viger Sta-

tion opened, Van Horne, making much of its French chateau origins, grandly dedicated it to "la gloire de la race canadienne-francaise."

Montreal's most famous station, however, was the CPR's Windsor Station. Designed by Bruce Price in 1886, the building was opened in 1889. Van Horne proudly proclaimed in six-foot letters that it "Beats All Creation, the New CPR Station." Edward Maxwell designed extensions to the station along the Rue la Gauchetière that nearly doubled the size of it. That and many other additions remained so true to the architectural style of the original structure that they are virtually indistinguish-ᵃble from it.

Shamed, in part, into action by the design for the Windsor Station, the Grand Trunk began in 1886 to replace its much criticized Bonaventure Station. In 1888 this Victorian style structure opened for business. Victorian arches, "chimneys," and cast iron around the tower roofs showed the GTR meant business. Inside, the GTR showed off a vaulted waiting room and an elegant dining room. But the beauty did not last. In 1916 a fire gutted much of the upper structure. Rather than re-build, the financially strapped railway simply removed the magnificent towers and turrets. In 1943 most passenger train service was re-moved to the new Gare Centrale. Following another fire in 1948, the sad old structure was replaced by a new freight and express complex.

Canada's third major railway line, the Canadian Northern, was soon to be heard from. In 1917 the railway that MacKenzie and Mann had built piecemeal from short lines here and there made its grand entrance into Montreal. On La Gauchetière Street, across the square from the Windsor Station, the CNo began erecting what was by comparison a utilitarian-looking station.

Passengers entered the classical station through five arched openings. The main wait-ing room contained oak benches, and the lay-out called for a men's smoking room and a women's waiting room. The main concourse and platforms were located on the lower level.

But the CNo was by then on the verge of bankruptcy, and soon afterwards the rugged little railway had become part of the govern-ment-operated Canadian National Railway system. The CNo's station was eventually re-placed by the Gare Centrale, designed by CNR architect John Schofield in 1943. The new

The Grand Trunk's Bonaventure Station foyer was one of the more beautiful of the day.

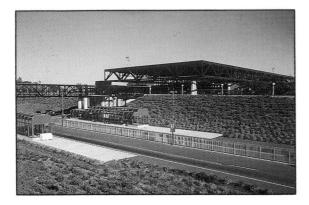

VIA's modern Ottawa station resembles more an airport. Located to be convenient to the suburbs and not to downtown, it was part of a major urban redesign undertaken during the 1960s by the National Capital Commission.

CPR's chateauesque Broad Street station was Ottawa's first Union station

National Archives of Canada PA 8676

building was a large but very plain representation of the early "modernist" style with its flat roof, straight lines, and ordinary windows. Now the major station for Via's passenger trains, Gare Centrale lies beneath the Queen Elizabeth Hotel on one side and the new CN headquarters on the other.

Ottawa

Before 1912, when Ottawa finally acquired a grand urban terminal that befitted its status as the nations's capital, it was a city of scattered nondescript little stations. The Canada Atlantic (absorbed by the Grand Trunk), the New York Central, the Canadian Northern, and the Bytown and Prescott all used small wooden stations or recycled buildings. In 1900, when the CPR opened its new Broad Street Station, Ottawa had its first architect-designed station (designed by CP's Edward Maxwell in his trademark chateau style).

Finally in 1912, the Grand Trunk opened its new Central Station on the site of the former military store that had been used as a station by the Canada Atlantic Railway. In 1920, when the CPR closed its Broad Street Station and moved in with the then-CNR, Central Station became Union Station.

Ottawa's current station resembles an airport terminal rather than a railway station. It is, however, easily accessible by public transport and well landscaped, recalling the old station gardens. Inside are a barber, tavern, gift shop, and car rental agencies, although with the government cutbacks in train service imposed in 1990, these facilities are closed most of the time.

Toronto

The first of Toronto's large urban stations was built by the Great Western Railway in 1857. Although not that company's largest urban terminal in Canada, its elegance was unsurpassed in its day. The prominent use of rounded arches and the emphasis on the train barn reflected a distinctly American influence, not surprising since that railway was American. However, when the Grand Trunk built Toronto's next grand urban palace in 1875, the Great Western joined in and abandoned its station over to the Grand Trunk for a produce storage. It eventually became a farmer's market, a use it retained until it burned in 1952.

Built in 1875, the new union station replaced a small board-and-batten building and was quickly proclaimed the grandest urban station on the continent. Although that may have been an overstatement, the station was indeed a grand structure. Constructed of stone and dominated by domes and Roman arches, it contained waiting rooms, offices, and a three-track train shed.

But within two decades Toronto had outgrown it. New rail yards and train sheds were added to the southern main entrance and completely obliterated its original beauty. A

Despite an addition , Toronto's domed 1873 station quickly became obsolete, its grandeur utterly obliterated by sprawling rail yards and new train sheds.

National Archives of Canada PA 87429

The cavernous great hall of Toronto's Union Station was designed to bring to mind the great hall in the Roman baths of Caracalla. Bas relief on the outside above the columns displays scenes of industrial Canada, dominated, naturally, by the railways. Etched on the inside are the names of Canada's major cities, railway destinations all.

The CPR's fanciful North Toronto station was built to rival the then proposed new Union Station. But by 1930 passenger service at the station remained at fewer than 10 trains per day (compared to 150 at the new union station), and the station was closed. In July 1940 it was reopened as a liquor store, a function that it retains today. Although the exterior still displays its remarkable charm, false walls and ceilings on the interior have completely covered the windows, the high ceiling, and the marble of the waiting room.

new entrance and offices were added to the north side, but they too proved inadequate. By 1900 the building had become obsolete.

The great fire of 1904 proved a blessing in disguise, at least for the Grand Trunk. By destroying much of downtown Toronto, the fire provided the Grand Trunk with the opportunity to lease one of the available sites and, in conjunction with the CPR, to begin to plan a new union station.

However, the GTR's dispute with the CPR over track elevation forestalled commencement, and in 1912 the CPR stalked out. Undaunted, in 1914 the Grand Trunk commissioned the Montreal architectural firm of Ross and MacDonald to devise plans for what would be one of the grandest railway stations in North America. Although construction was almost complete in 1919, political wrangling delayed the opening until 1927, and even then the building wasn't entirely complete. For two more years passengers were required to walk from the new concourse to the old platforms.

The culmination of what architects call the "beaux arts" style, Toronto's Union Station features a row of soaring Greek columns.

Although the acrimonious dispute with the CPR delayed Union Station's construction, it did produce one unexpected benefit: another architectural gem, the CPR's North Toronto, or Summerhill, Station.

When the CPR hammered a new route to Smiths Falls into the ground in 1913 and crossed Yonge Street at Summerhill, about one and a half miles north of Union Station, it built a small station on the west of the street that it called "Yorkville." In 1916 the skyline was dramatically reformed when a spectacular new limestone building, italian-

Metro Toronto Reference Library

ate in design and dominated by a fifty-metre clock tower, was opened. The CPR was not used to playing second fiddle to the Grand Trunk and built the handsome new union station (it was to be shared with Canadian Northern) to preemptively challenge the dominance of the Grand Trunk's new station, which was still being designed. Designed by the Toronto architectural firm of Darling and Pearson, it contained bas relief motifs on the outside, while three arching windows stretched the full thirty-foot height of the waiting room and shed ribbons of light that reflected on the floors and walls of brown and green marble.

Unfortunately, the new station was in the wrong place at the wrong time. When it opened in 1927, the new union station could more than handle increased passenger traffic, whereas a change to a train at the CPR North Toronto Station meant a long and inconvenient trip along a crowded Yonge Street.

By 1930 passenger service at the North Toronto Station remained at fewer than 10 trains per day (compared to 150 at the new union station), and the station was closed. In July 1940 it was reopened as a liquor store, a function that it retains today.

Proposals by CPR's Marathon Realty for new development on the lands adjacent to the station call for preserving the grand old building. Torontonians hope that they also call for restoring the interior to its original and eloquent beauty.

Hamilton

Hamilton, Ontario, lost two early monuments, that of the GTR (a former Great Western station) and the original Italianate

The original Toronto Hamilton and Buffalo station in Hamilton Ontario was removed when grade separation was needed at the crossing.

Toronto, Hamilton and Buffalo, but gained in their place two perhaps equally appealing monuments, the neo-classical station of the CNR and the art deco station of the TH and B.

The TH and B style is found in no other Canadian station. Designed by the New York firm of Fellheimer and Wagner, it was built in 1933. Modified from a more elaborate design, the six-storey tower was headquarters for the company. The wider two-storey base displays curved wrap-around windows. The waiting room impressed passengers with modern features, terrazzo floors, and central light-

ing fixtures. Passengers entered from the street and boarded the train from the second floor. At the time of writing the building sits vacant. The platform, canopies yet in place, is cracked and overgrown with weeds, a sorry state for such a memorable station.

The Hamilton CNR station enjoys happier circumstances. One of a series designed by CN architect John Schofield, it was built in 1930 and features a neo-classical facade punctu-

Ontario's oldest non-Grand Trunk station sits in St. Thomas, Ontario. It has been designated for preservation under the new federal government legislation to protect railway stations.

(right) The union station, Cochrane, Ontario.

ated by Greek columns and portico. The wide lawn that lies in front of the building is a rare element of landscape that has given way to parking lots at most of Canada's urban stations. As in many stations of the 1920s, the entrance features bas relief images of railway transportation. The building remains in use, hosting Via, Amtrack, and GO trains.

* * *

Many of Canada's other towns and cities contain urban monuments of their own: the beautiful red sandstone office and former station of the Algoma Central Railway in Sault Ste Marie; the Ross and MacDonald creation for the CPR at Trois Rivières, Quebec, with its surprisingly minuscule classical entrance;

and the E and N (CPR) station at Nanaimo, B.C., built in 1920 and likely designed by divisional engineer R.A. Bainbridge.

Canadian cities need not be big to warrant a monumental station. The former Penn Central station in Windsor and the one-time Michigan Central station in St. Thomas, both in Ontario, are elegant examples of American railway architecture. The brick station in Windsor, built by the Michigan Central in 1911, with its Dutch gables is strongly reminiscent of the Intercolonial Railway station in Pictou. The former Canada Southern station in St. Thomas must rank as one of the longest stations in Canada. Designed by Canada Southern architect E. Barryman, it was built in 1873 and is the oldest non–Grand Trunk station in Ontario.

The two-storey stone station in North Bay, Ontario, with its wide, arched windows, has presided over the CPR yards since 1903, while at nearby Sudbury a smaller passenger station renovated by Via Rail before the Mulroney cutbacks nestles beside the larger but plainer CP offices and divisional station. The CN/ONR union station in Cochrane, Ontario, while stripped of its handsome gables and cupola, remains that town's most prominent building and its historic *raison d'etre*. Likewise, Churchill, Manitoba's, station (1942), although not old, has, with its steep roof and hip gables, captured fully and eloquently the chateau lines of Canadian station architecture of a half century earlier.

The CPR's London, Ontario, station, designed by Bruce Price in 1887 and with a mixture of chateau and Tudor Revival styles, is the sole survivor of the era when London could claim five stations (including its original Great Western station and the ornate but long-forgotten Michigan Central station built as a terminus for its London and Port Stanley line). Although Canada retains many of its urban monuments, it has lost far too many. Moncton contained a widely acclaimed red brick station that, with its steep rooflines, was reminiscent of the chateau tradition. It was destroyed in the 1960s by the CN and replaced with a faceless modern structure.

Thunder Bay

Thunder Bay originally was two cities, Port Arthur and Fort William. A major grain transshipment site for the CPR and the Canadian Northern, as well the later Grand Trunk Pacific, both Fort William and Port Arthur contained a half dozen stations.

The most striking was the one in Port Arthur designed by R.B. Pratt and built by the Canadian Northern in 1905. Its size and its unique design, however, set it completely apart from anything the CNo had done before or since.

Meanwhile, on the other side of town, Fort William, the CPR reigned supreme. In 1910, as the Grand Trunk Pacific rolled into town, the CPR moved out of a smaller pattern-book station and into a three-storey brick building with a flat roof and a few architectural embellishments that it shared with its rival. (At this point the GTP was not a through line, but rather a branch line from its main line further north.)

In Port Arthur the CPR operated an attrac-

tive but smaller station of brick and stone built in 1907 directly across the track from that of the CNo. The building was dominated by a massive tower that was noticeably out of scale with the smaller waiting room and offices. All the original CPR structures in Thunder Bay have been demolished.

The former CNo station is no longer used by the railway and now houses retail outlets. It remains a stunning centrepiece for Thunder Bay's renovated waterfront. The Fort William station remains in use by the railway.

Winnipeg

Virtually all lines west passed through Winnipeg. Often called the "Chicago of the North" (perhaps we should call Chicago the "Winnipeg of the South"), Winnipeg owes its existence to the railways. The railways in turn built stations here that are among the classics of the country.

In 1888 the CPR built in Winnipeg the largest station in western Canada. According to a contemporary traveller, the "large and handsome station was worthy of a metropolitan city like Winnipeg," but within a decade even that building was due to be replaced by a larger, chateau-style station. Haggling over the price of land delayed construction long enough for the CPR to change its mind and opt instead for the current trend in station architecture, the beaux arts style. The architects were the familiar W.S. and E. Maxwell.

In 1904 the large red brick building with its Greek columns replaced the old station. Adjoining the station the CPR added the Royal Alexandra Hotel. The hotel has been demolished but the station survives and, inside, the

Long gone and largely forgotten is the London Ontario terminus of the former London and Port Stanley Railway

CN's former Port Arthur (Thunder Bay) station. Its two steep pyramidal roofs displayed the chateauesque roofline sported by even the CNo's smaller stations, while beneath the gables the CNo added concrete wheatsheafs, a tribute to the railway's western customers.

CP's Winnipeg station was part of a complex that included the now-demolished Royal Alexandra Hotel. The station is a federally designated historic station.

Regina's Union station sadly sits vacant in this 1990 photo.

The chateauesque touch of Canadian Northern architect R.B. Pratt is evident on this, Saskatoon's second CNo station.

waiting room, dim and dusty, still displays its 1930s fixtures.

Winnipeg did, however, end up with a chateau station, if only for a short time—the Northern Pacific's "Winnipeg Hotel." Seven storeys high and with the steep roofs that typified the chateau style, it was designed by architect C.E. Joy, who incorporated the station on the ground floor. The building was short-lived, burning in 1899.

In 1911 the CNo built what it called its Fort Garry Union Station in conjunction with the GTP. It was designed by the New York firm of Warren and Wetmore and used an oversized archway to emphasize the railway's role as the gateway to the city. Capped by a dome, the waiting room soars eighty-eight feet and is wainscotted with marble. The architects used natural light to illuminate both offices and waiting room alike. Because Winnipeg was a major immigrant distribution point, the railway incorporated special food and bath facilities for immigrants on the basement level.

Brandon

Brandon was one of those cities that earned its grand stations through the size and vitality of the city alone, for it lacked the specialized railway functions that fuelled places like Winnipeg and Fort William/Port Arthur.

Here in 1911 the CNo built a stub line from its main line into the town, where it built an impressive brick station with a hotel attached. Nearby on the CPR main line in the same year, a small classic station replaced the earlier station.

The track to the CN station was lifted in 1970, and the station is now a popular lounge. The CPR station saw daily passenger traffic until the Conservative government of Brian Mulroney stripped the country of much of its badly needed rail service and left the Brandon CPR station without passengers for the first time in eighty years.

Regina

In 1892 CP architect Edward Colonna designed a single storey, red brick station for Regina, one that was distinguished by a squat but prominent tower. Like so many other stations of the period, it quickly proved too small.

Regina's attractive union station, which reflected the Italian Renaissance mood that swept the railway world after the turn of the century, was designed by the CPR and built jointly by the CPR and CNo in 1911. The GTP operated a smaller station nearby until 1920, when it was absorbed into the CNR monolith. The station was extensively renovated in 1930, an alteration that removed the Italian Renaissance appearance and replaced it with the then current art deco style. Only the trackside entrance retained the earlier style. Today it stands empty thanks to the government rail passenger cutbacks, bereft of its passengers and awaiting proposals for reuse.

Saskatoon

Saskatoon has gone through a surprising number of stations. The oldest was built by the CPR in its chateau style, a copy of those in Strathcona (Edmonton) and Kenora. The Grand Trunk Pacific in 1913 added a two-storey wooden station, and the Canadian Northern used the architectural wizardry of R.B. Pratt to design one of his chateau stations, a style nearly identical to that used in Dauphin.

Both these old structures were replaced in the 1930s when the CN built a simpler, flat-roofed station of brick and concrete. Although the classical details were gone, the strong entrance way continued to reflect the railways' obsession with "gateway." But even this station was demolished in the 1960s, when the CN added its modern-era station on the outskirts of the city. The CPR station, however, still survives.

Edmonton

Like its sister cities on the prairies, Edmonton went through several generations of stations. Here too the talents of R. B. Pratt created for the Canadian Northern Railway a chateau-style station that was a near duplicate of the CPR's Broad Street Station in Ottawa. The Grand Trunk Pacific used the station as well.

In March 1928 the CN opened, to much fanfare, its new station. CN architect John Schofield chose to combine utility and beauty and came up with a "simple but dignified front," according to the *Edmonton Bulletin*. The main floor contained a large waiting room illuminated by skylights, and off to the

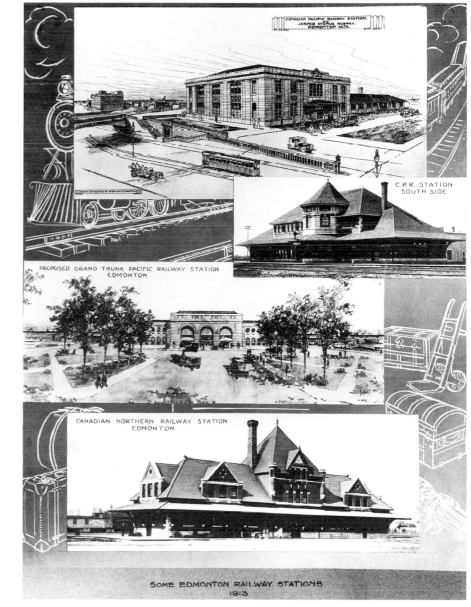

Provincial Archives of Alberta A 4690

Of the 4 Edmonton stations shown in this collage only the CPR "South Side" or Strathcona station survives.

The Canadian Northern bought this building, which had been a boy's school, to serve as its first Calgary station.

side a dining room and restaurant. "Edmonton may well be proud of her new station," concluded the *Bulletin*.

Meanwhile, the CPR, denied entrance into Edmonton, had at first to content itself with its chateau station in Strathcona on the south shore of the river. Finally, in 1913 with the long-awaited bridge finished, the CPR built a flat-roofed classical station in downtown Edmonton. Costing two hundred thousand dollars, the station contained, in addition to the usual ticketing and waiting rooms, a special immigrants' waiting room tucked into the basement. "The new station, yards, depot, and freight shed proclaim the company's faith in the future importance of Edmonton," lauded the *Edmonton Bulletin*.

Despite the praise of the day, both Edmonton stations have been demolished. The CN's was replaced in 1966 by the modern office tower known as the "CN Tower," and the CPR's was demolished in 1978 despite the earnest efforts of the local citizenry to save it. Ironically, the oldest of them all, the station at Strathcona, still survives.

Calgary

Predominantly a CPR town, Calgary went though four stations in less than twenty-five years. From its first temporary station, a boxcar, Calgary acquired a Van Horne and then five years later a single-storey sandstone structure designed by CPR architect Thomas Corolla. But Calgary was growing so quickly that the new station was soon obsolete, and in 1911 it was replaced with a larger classical station that incorporated a low archway in place of the more usual Greek columns.

As in Edmonton, the Calgary station was submerged in the 1960s craze to depersonalize downtown Canada with faceless office towers. In 1969 the CPR's Palliser Square opened in downtown Calgary; with its towers and gleaming offices, the new development relegated the station to a small area in the basement.

Vancouver

Until the mid-1960s Vancouver was the only city in Canada that could count three massive classical stations. That of the CPR, designed by Barrott, Blackadar and Webster of Montreal, sports a row of gleaming white columns in front of a large red office building. In the waiting room were models of Canadian Pacific steamships and scenic oil paintings in the frieze. Built in 1914, this station replaced one of Canada's most magnificent but shortest-lived chateau stations, designed by none other than Edward Maxwell. It was demolished in 1914, just sixteen years after it was built, to make way for the new station.

The two other classical stations stood side by side. The Great Northern station was designed by Vancouver architect Fred Townley and built in 1915. A union station, for it housed the Northern Pacific as well, it was distinguished by not one but two arched entrance ways.

Meanwhile, next door Canadian Northern architect R.B. Pratt was turning his skills to the classical mode, designing a station that, although it contained only one arched entrance, was equally attractive. The building featured lunch counters and a dining room, as well as a barber shop, drug store, and

(above) Classic arches and red brick distinguish Vancouver's CP station.

(below) CN's classic Vancouver terminal, along with that of the CPR, gives that city two magnificent stations.

YWCA Travellers' Aid office. In the 1950s the Great Northern transferred its passenger traffic to the CN station, and in 1964, to avoid high land taxes, demolished its classical station.

Victoria

The terminus of the Esquimalt and Nanaimo Railway, Victoria had only one urban palace. A small but delightful Italianate station, it was built of red brick and was distinguished by a series of arches. In 1947 the CPR added a second floor, and then in 1972 demolished it entirely. Its replacement was an appalling concrete-block box located several blocks from the centre of town. In 1985 Via Rail built on the site of the original station a small but pleasing waiting room for its island service. Constructed of brick and topped with a steeply pitched roof, it represents a modern return to traditional railway style.

Prince Rupert

Prince Rupert, thought the executives of the Grand Trunk Pacific, was destined to surpass Vancouver as the shipping centre of the West Coast, and they designed a station to fit. They hired former CP architect Francis Rattenbury, designer of a number of hotels, to design a monumental chateau-like station.
Rattenbury's plan depicted a station with two turrets and an arch overlooking the water. Beside it would be a grand hotel with 450 rooms. He proposed large gardens and wide tree-lined boulevards. The cost would be a staggering $2 million.

Unfortunately, the glorious port fizzled, and the station remained a dream and a hole in the ground. A much smaller station was built, and the excavation for the dream station ended up as a pool and a fountain. In 1975 it was filled in for a shopping centre, and the site of the proposed lawn and gardens is now a parking lot.

***

Having weathered redundancy and threats of demolition, many of Canada's urban stations survive. Despite senseless rail passenger cutbacks, many are still gateways for arriving train passengers—the Halifax, Quebec, Toronto, Winnipeg, and Vancouver stations still cling to that function. For most travelling Canadians, however, their "gateway" is the airport, their first view of their destination is one of lineups, traffic, and tedious highway "strip" development. Although it was largely for corporate self-glorification, the railway station builders at least gave Canadians a sense of grand arrival, of importance and self-esteem as they walked through the looming archway or the towering columns, and found the city at their beckoning. It is a value today's transportation architects would do well to adopt.

The Masters of the Station:

The Railway Station Agents

They once numbered in the tens of thousands and, according to some, were the most influential men (only a few were women) in small-town Canada, more prominent than bankers and politicians, and the envy of the clergy. According to others, the agents were surly and self-serving, more concerned about rules, forms, and freight receipts, than they were about the comfort and convenience of passengers. But revered or reviled, the railway station agent, like the station he manned, has vanished from the roll call of Canadian communities.

Before construction began on the Great Western Railway in 1851, Canada's rail lines consisted of only a handful of portage railways: the Erie and Ontario, the Montreal and Lachine, and the Champlain and St. Lawrence. Because these lines transported only passengers and a bit of freight from one waterway to another, the agents' early assignments were relatively straightforward. Like those on the stage coach and canal operations that preceded them, their first jobs were to ticket passengers, collect freight bills, and drum up business for the railway. But unlike stage coaches and steamers, trains operated in two directions, usually along a single track, generating a new function: making sure that trains didn't collide.

Before the telegraph and before standard time, that wasn't easy. No two communities had the same hour on their clocks at the same time; trains operated as best they could according to a simple timetable. All trains were required to stop while engineers reported to the station agent to sign the train order forms. If the train ahead had been late, the agent held up the train at hand until he assumed the previous train was clear. With no telegraph or other form of inter-station communication, he simply held his breath and hoped he was right.

However, by 1855 the Grand Trunk and Great Western railways had become Canada's first main lines; the telegraph was making train operations simpler and safer, and relaying train orders soon became the agents' most important function.

As orders would click in from the dispatcher in the divisional station, the agent had to carefully write them down. Because this task took up such a large portion of the agent's time, sending and receiving telegraph messages became almost second nature. It was not uncommon for an agent to send a telegram with one hand while writing a letter with the other. Some agents might even boast of reading a book, writing a letter, and carrying on a conversation all while sending a telegram. They were, however, unlikely to try such juggling acts with the all-important train orders.

Agents kept order in the chaotic coming and going of trains and made sure that the distances between them were safe. In the fall, when grain and farm products had to be shipped quickly or perish, trains puffed past main-line stations often at twenty-minute intervals. A mistake of mere minutes meant the difference between life and death. On December 26, 1902, the crack passenger train the Chicago Flyer, blinded by an early blizzard, roared through the Watford, Ontario, station

without receiving orders. Ahead, manoeuvring to get onto a siding and out of the way of the onrushing Flyer, was a slow freight train. Had the Flyer stopped for orders it might have averted disaster. Instead it smashed into the freight, killing the engineer, firemen, and thirty-eight passengers.

Another bane of the agents were the hated silk trains. In 1924 the newly created Canadian National Railways won the coveted silk run contract. The job was to get Japanese silk from Vancouver to New York before the living cocoons, worms, and mulberry leaves that made up the valuable shipment began to deteriorate. Spurred on by the high cost of insuring the shipments, the CNR pulled out all the stops to get the shipments across the country as quickly as possible. As the trains stopped only briefly at divisional points, the agents had to clear the track ahead for the highballing silk train. All freight and passenger trains had to be safely on sidings well in advance.

In 1924 one silk train roared across the continent from Vancouver to Prescott, a distance of twenty-eight hundred miles, in just eighty-one hours and ten minutes. On May 15, 1940, nylon stockings were introduced onto the market with great fanfare. By the end of the Second World War nylon had largely replaced silk, and the silk trains became a fading bad memory for the agents

that handled them.

Train ordering was just one of the agent's many duties. Lorne Perry of the CN writes, "They had to be masters of many trades. They handled and remitted money, collected accounts, ordered supplies, tended the garden, handled telegrams and money orders and kept track of goods awaiting pick-up or shipment."

It was not surprising, then, that the railways were often accused of heaping too much work on the solitary agents. In 1908, when the Post Office tried to urge the railways to add mail-side delivery to the growing list of agents' duties, their union, the Order of Railroad Telegraphers, resisted. "They are being overworked, and...it [is] a physical impossibility...to undertake any more duties," pleaded union vice-president D. Campbell. "Practically every Agent...west of Fort William was urged to assume the mail-side delivery," he went on. This, combined with the "manipulation of gates at some distance from the office, and performances of clerical work...[were] too great a multiplicity of duties." Then there was the grain work. "The agents," quotes Campbell, "are required to deliver to each farmer the necessary amount of [seed grain]...[and without] any additional assistance, the work had to be done in a very few days."

All the extra duties were heaped on the

agents without any increase in staff. "Just at the time that the responsibility in handling train orders is greatest, the excessive burden of the numerous duties also occurs.... Telegraph operators or agents should not be overtaxed with a multiplicity of other duties.... Train dispatchers...should not be burdened with the mechanical work of continually compiling statements and reports not necessary to the movement of trains." Complaints by employees, added Campbell, were countered with threats of dismissal.

Grain duties didn't get any easier as time went on. In 1960, W.S. Beaton, a district inspector for the Board of Transport Commissioners of Canada (formerly the Board of Railway Commissioners), listed no fewer than 28 separate duties that the agent must

perform when handling grain. These included sending daily wires of empty grain cars needed; filling out forms; billing and sending cars; sending daily telegraphic car reports, daily revenue reports, and daily yard checks (by mail); preparing switch lists and way bills; and keeping records of which cars went to which elevator. If this wasn't enough, the agent had to tally most of the daily paper work each month. Not only was the agent responsible for his own station, but for unmanned flag stations as well.

Passenger bookings were another of the agent's more important tasks. When railways expanded into the tourist business with hotels and steamships, the agent became a travel agent and made bookings that might be a simple one-way fare to the next town or

a world-wide excursion that included several steamer and train connections.

In addition, the agent solicited freight business. In towns where more than one railway existed and competition was fierce, the job required particular tact and salesmanship. Agents supervised the loading and unloading of shipments and made sure the bills were paid. Not all freight shipments were easy. Clayton Cook of Newfoundland, the son of an agent at Princeton, Newfoundland, remembers the cattle. "Should there be a shipment of cattle," he recalls, "[my Dad] would have to, in addition to his station duties, feed and water the cattle and clean the mess." That job might last until the cattle train was ready to move the animals on to their destination, or until the owner came to claim them,

Provincial Archives of Alberta A 4646

Freight waiting to be shipped at Olds, Alberta, ca. 1904; keeping track of shipments was one of the agent's most time-consuming tasks.

which might involve a wait of "sometimes...several days," according to Mr. Cook.

When railways entered the commercial telegraph business, the agent became responsible for sending and receiving messages and money orders. Because the agent was a banker of sorts, the railways provided the stations with safes, bars on the ticket windows, and sturdy locks. The rule books were firm; no one was allowed into the ticket office for any reason. In addition to all their other duties, many agents were post masters as well. When the mail train arrived the agent would sort the letters and magazines and then pass them to the small but eager crowd waiting. In Canada only those communities too small for separate post offices were given post offices in the stations. However, in Newfound-

land during the depression the small post offices were given to the agents all along the line, a chore that lasted until Newfoundland's confederation with Canada in 1949.

Railway rule books reminded the agents not only of their duties but also of their role in the community. "The local agent is the railway's front-line contact with the public," notes the CNR rule book. "To many he is the railway." As a result, much of the rule book is devoted to station appearance. Even the least appealing of an agent's household chores were spelled out in detail. "Particular attention should be directed to keeping the toilets as clean as possible. These places should be frequently washed, adding a small quantity of suitable disinfectant [phenolic emulsifiable disinfectant was recommended]." The rule

Waiting room, North Toronto station. As the CNR rule book put it, "stations should always be kept clean and tidy. A clean, tidy station creates immediately a favourable impression on our passengers and patrons. The waiting room should be kept free from dust and rubbish. Frequent sweeping and dusting and a periodic washing of the floors should be carried out."

book didn't stop there: "Attention should be paid to the toilet bowls," it goes on. "Sometimes these become discoloured and very repulsive looking, often giving off an objectionable odour." No wonder the agents spent so much time in their gardens.

Often the agent's role was like that of a king ruling over a small domain. He played a key role in the everyday life of the community. According to Lorne Perry of the CNR, his was "a respected job, and in some cases the station agent was the best paid person in town." In smaller, less sophisticated farm towns he might share the spotlight with such other civic luminaries as the elevator manager, the pool hall operator, the tavern owner, or the part-time preacher.

If the town was located on a busy line, one that had several telegraph wires, the agent was its source of news. Clayton Cook recalls how his father would copy all the news from the wire and place it on a special bulletin board for members of the community to read.

Whenever a special sports event occurred, the agent became announcer, long before radio. Donald Leslie, agent at Troup Junction in British Columbia, recalls in his lengthy and eloquent memoirs the night of the world boxing championship fight between Jack Johnson and Tommy Burns in Australia. "It was suggested...that I should copy the fight story off the press wire, handing [it] out the window round by round, and that one of the

CN Archives X-50363-C

The Brockville Ontario agent waters his garden — one of the more enjoyable of an agent's duties.

men would announce it as the account came in." Excitement soared as the fight neared its climax, the crowd favourite, Burns, finally losing. "The audience solaced itself with assorted beverages, but the announcer was too busy announcing so he could not participate, and he tried to catch up when the fight finished and swallowed too much in too short a time...he fell off one of the moored barges into deep water instead of stepping into his boat and we had quite a session getting him aboard."

Nelson concludes, "Before radio this was standard procedure for all major sporting events such as the World Series and always at election times."

In 1909 telephones were finally introduced to the railway stations. Bowing to pressure from the Peoples Telephone Company and the Caledon Telephone Company, the Board of Railway Commissioners required the railways to allow telephone companies to install phones in the stations. But as the agent was the only person permitted to use the phone, and the station phone was often the only one in many small towns, it was just one more job for the overworked agents. Many resisted. In 1911 the Renfrew Mercury complained that the K and P agent at Calabogie, Ontario was demanding payment to answer the phone, while in Quebec the Bonaventure and Gaspé Telephone Company raged that agents were refusing to answer the phone at all. But gradually the telephone was accepted and soon became a vital news link to what was still the "outside" world.

Not all the news was good. During the wars the agent, often having the only telephone in town, was called upon to relay the news of a son or husband killed overseas.

The phone operator would contact the agent, and as soon as the operator advised him that it was the "Defense Department," the agent knew that he once more had to tell one of his families that a member would not be coming home.

If the agent was the news link, he was often the emergency link as well. Mrs. Ollie Bertie of Taber, Alberta, recalls the role that her station in Beaver Brook, New Brunswick, played in emergencies: "If there was an accident or any emergency we depended on the stationmaster. The phone in the office of the station was strictly a railway phone. You could talk only to other station masters on it. In any kind of emergency the station master in Beaver Brook would have to get in touch with the station master in whatever town you were calling and then he would have to make the call for you."

Clayton Cook notes that his father saved more than one life. Whenever a villager would fall ill, he would arrange to have the section foreman transport the patient on his track motorcar the eighteen miles to the nearest doctor.

Sometimes there was no time to travel to the doctor or to wait for one. As a result, many small-town babies were born in the local station, with the agent or his wife performing midwife functions. One former agent claims to have delivered fourteen babies before the doctor could arrive.

To the young men of early Canada the call of the railway was irresistible, a lure of romance and adventure. Many young boys spent their free summer hours down at the station helping the agent load and unload freight, and learning to read the semaphore. Then, when they were old enough, they

CP Corporate Archives A 7632

The agent, J.P. Phelan, is third from the left in this photo taken with Dominion Express Managers outside the Port Moody station.

would hire on. Most began as clerks, working their way to telegraph operator, and then finally bidding on the coveted job as full-fledged agent.

Many yearned to be agents long before they were old enough. E. Stanley Johnson wrote in the CP *Staff Bulletin* in 1943 how he hungered for a railway position. "You're only fourteen!" exclaimed the agent. "That's pretty young for a form clerk." " 'Well,' said I, 'for one thing there's nobody else around here can do it. For another I'm mighty quick at figuring'.... There was a CPR rule that no man could become a train order telegrapher until he was nineteen...but finally came my birthday. Nineteen years old! It was the most glorious day of my life and I celebrated it by

setting out on the road as a [station] telegraph operator."

Donald Leslie, when applying for a job as station agent, was a little less scrupulous. "I was asked how old I was and I countered with the question 'How old must I be?' Eighteen was the required minimum to hold the position of railway agent, so I deducted three years from 1894 and appeared on the staff records as having been born in 1891."

One of the youngest of all was Hugh Neilson who, as telegraph operator in the Great Western Railway station in St. Catharines, Ontario, left a remarkable diary of station life in 1861. "After having been on the job for a month," he noted in his diary, "I will be fourteen years old on the 18th of this month."

For most stations the agent was the telegraph operator. But at busier stations a special night operator was often used, while at others a full-time telegraph operator was on duty even days to relieve the agent.

Other than memorizing the rule book; learning waybilling, accounting, and ticketing; and spending hours on the telegraph key, there was little training for station agents. The biggest hurdle was waiting in line for a vacancy. "Employees bid on jobs," according to Lorne Perry of the CNR, "according to seniority, so the lonely night jobs were for the newcomers. Prized jobs were for those with the opportunity for commission in addition to salary, for telegraph, money orders, express."

Although rare, some agents were private operators. The London and Port Stanley Railroad, when first opened, did not have telegraph facilities, and agents at such secondary stations as Westminster, Glanworth, and White's simply leased the stations from the railroad.

The life of an agent could be crushingly uneventful. "Life at Troup was dull really," recalls Leslie. "I had been used to hearing intelligent conservation at home.... Now I had no one at all except for a brief moment or two when the two trains went through and a freight train at two- or three-day intervals." He sought ways to fill those empty hours. "At night I played telegraphic chess with the night operator up at Kaslo but neither of us was very good at it."

Hugh Neilson complained frequently in his diary of having little to do, and filled much of his account with the difficulties of borrowing books. "I have been lying on the sofa nearly all day sleeping," he wrote on one particularly dull day. "Not much doing."

But on a main line like that of the Great Western through St. Catharines, life did not stay dull for long. "Have been busy in the office today," writes Neilson the very next day. "Lots of specials and pilots coming and going...trains all very late...train west didn't come until 9:45. It was late when we went to bed."

Whenever a dignitary passed through, all hands were put on alert. "Father got a message today saying we must be on hand with operator to make arrangements for a special passenger train with the Honourable John Ross, Inspector of Public Works, going to Toronto," Neilson wrote, added sardonically, "That will be another thin dollar for me this month."

The hours were long. Neilson opened his station at 6:30 in the morning and remained on duty until 8 at night. Bad weather or extra traffic sometimes kept him on duty until midnight. Sundays were the only holiday; paid vacation was unheard of.

Pay for operators was about a dollar a day, and from that the agents had to pay the railway five dollars a month for accommodation. A divisional stationmaster in charge of a large staff received seventy-five a month. To earn this they worked ten hours a day for six days a week. With monthly pay, overtime pay did not exist.

To help compensate for the lack of overtime pay, agents earned commissions from handling Dominion Express Company work, selling land for the company's Land Department, sending commercial telegrams, or, as one agent in Lindsay, Ontario, did, teaching telegraphing school.

The agent's job was not all rosy. J.A. Hamelin, night operator at MacLeod, Alberta, provides this rare insight into the less pleasant aspects of station work. Testifying at the hearing of the stations regular operator, he lamented, "a night operator has to work twelve hours every day.... I worked all the night before last and yesterday there was a big dance at the hotel [hotels were almost invariably right behind the station, and often "home" for station operators not living at the station]...the hotel was full of people dancing and making noise, and consequently I could not sleep, and then I had to get ready for another 12 hour shift. I don't think," he concluded, "a man can do a 12 hour shift without sleep." Then, asked how many consecutive days he had worked without a holiday, Hamelin replied, "I have been working nearly every day for three years,...Sundays and all."

A task many dreaded was hooping up orders to an oncoming steam engine in the black of the night. Another was substituting for off-duty agents, a chore that was made more onerous in the 1950s when the forty-hour week replaced the sixty-hour week, requiring more substitutions than ever before.

Then there was the hated ritual known as bumping. This occurred whenever an agent with more seniority bumped a more junior agent from his station and replaced him. The agent that was displaced could in turn bump an agent still more junior, and set in motion a domino process that could a upset an entire division.

Writing in B.C. Rail's employee publication *Remembering*, Don McKinnon recalls how he bumped a local contractor, a move that proved somewhat unpopular with the contractor's fellow villagers. "In 1947 the railway decided to open the Pemberton station and I bid on the position and got it. At that time the railway had a contract person handling the shipments. He was a nice gentleman and was performing the job well...it didn't go over well with the people in the valley. It wasn't really difficult or unpleasant, it was just lonely."

Generally, however, the railways rewarded loyalty. A CPR agent in Tweed, Ontario, when too old to continue with his heavier duties, was transferred to a larger sta

The agent at work, Canadian Northern station, Boissevain, Manitoba, ca. 1912.

The Toronto, Hamilton and Buffalo station, Mount Pleasant. Flag stations like this relied on agents at nearby stations or on caretaker agents.

tion where for the same salary he carried more specialized lighter duties. At Kaladar, Ontario, the CPR paid an agent two hundred and fifty dollars that he had missed in wages while attending to family problems.

Disputes between agents and maintenance crews were not uncommon. While agents were responsible for interior maintenance, the maintenance workers looked after the exterior. "There was a man fell through the platform," complained Elgin, Ontario, agent M. Boses to his divisional superintendent. "Although he was not hurt he might have been. I have repaired it temporarily but if they [the maintenance crew] do not repair platforms I

have no lumber to repair them.... Please see what can be done and oblige."

Stubborn supervisors occasionally made an agents's life unpleasant. When Hugh Neilson planned to visit his sister in Kansas he had to secure permission from his superior, one Dwight, but found that getting it took longer than he had anticipated. "Telegraphed to Dwight asking if he had received my letter and if he could grant my request," and two days later the despairing Neilson wrote in his diary: "This was the morning I expected to leave for Kansas but as I have heard nothing from Dwight and no one sent in my place, I couldn't leave." He finally received his leave, but his troubles didn't end there. After he returned, his replacement, O'Donohoe, departed leaving a few unpaid debts. "O'Donohoe went west today on Day Express. It seems he didn't pay all his board at Knapps. He owes one week yet and it's doubtful if they will ever get it."

Receiving his own pay presented Neilson with further problems. "Smith [his paymaster] is going to fetch up [his twenty-four dollars] today sometime. I guess he is afraid I or my father will speak to Dwight about it...he is going to pay me regular after this month."

Agents had to adhere strictly to the rule books, and any deviation invited demerit points. According to the April 1937 educational bulletin for the southern Ontario district of the CNR, more than fifty-five employees, including agents, received demerit points. Some of the infractions included "failure to punch ticket 'baggage checked', 5 points; delay to correspondence, 5 points; responsibility for passenger missing train connection, 5 points; error in billing, 10 points." By contrast, only eight individuals earned merits.

More serious problems such as drunkenness were dealt with more severely. Marty Young, agent at Nokomis, Manitoba, remembered the night in 1907 when the RCMP awakened him to check on his night operator. He hurried down to a waiting room full of people and found the operator asleep.

"I ticketed as many [people] as time would permit," he later recalled. "I was about to try and awaken the operator when he staggered to his feet and said he was going to bed.... The next night he came in drunk and out for trouble.... I told him to go home and sleep it off...he refused so I pointed to the door and began taking off my coat. After a brief bout I ejected him and as he was being propelled through the door he grabbed the wall phone and took it along with a spot of plaster." This story, however, ended on a happier note. "The next night he came on duty in good fettle and from that night on he was as good as any man I ever worked with."

The depression of the thirties brought the agents some unexpected problems—hobos. Desperate for work, any work, they would illegally ride freight cars from town to town looking for a job. On cold nights they would sleep in the baggage room of the nearest station, often with the unspoken approval of the agent. Most agents sympathized with the hobos, and some would bring them a meal in exchange for light labour. Ernie Boyd of Ompah, Ontario, remembers his father allowing one itinerant to bed down in the Lavant, Ontario, station waiting room one Christmas. In exchange, the traveller, who had some magical talent and played violin, performed for the local community Christmas party.

Although the job of agent was an almost exclusively male domain, many women filled in during the Second World War when Canada's young men went to Europe to fight. The arrival of ladies evoked different reactions among the remaining males. The most common was the temptation to play jokes. At the Ignace station in northwestern Ontario, the new female employees arrived in their assigned record room apprehensive but ready to work. The veteran male employees seemed serious enough, and the new ladies assumed the transition would proceed smoothly. Then they opened their desks to find the drawers filled with young snakes.

Break-ins were infrequent, but during the 1920s a rash of break-ins plagued a number of rural stations around Toronto. The agent at Don rigged a rope from the door to the telegraph so that the night operator along the line would be alerted of a break-in. Shortly thereafter the booby trap caught the culprits, and the agent received ten merit marks.

Another station operator, however, was fired for his inventiveness. American inventor Thomas Alva Edison had become night operator at St. Mary's Junction in Ontario. Because the nights saw few trains, night operators were required to send the dispatcher the codeword "six" every half hour to show they were awake. But the youthful inventor, possibly because he was hard of hearing, devised an apparatus that automatically tripped the telegraph while he napped. To his shock, one night he found that a train order had arrived, he had missed it, and the train had passed. A frantic call to the next operator prevented what might have a disastrous wreck. And so, Edison's career as a Canadian station agent ended abruptly.

Algonquin Park Museum 73

Isolation was hard on families like this one in Algonquin Park's remote and often isolated Canoe Lake station.

On occasion, agents found themselves in the middle of larger disputes. In 1891, when the Toronto, Hamilton and Buffalo, then just assembling its lines, purchased the older Brantford, Waterford and Lake Erie Railway, the directors of the latter became impatient with the former's late payment. They tried to hasten the outstanding debt by taking back their railway by force. After seizing a locomotive at West Brantford, they decided next to seize the station. When the station agent, one Mr. Nelles, tried to defend the station, the BW and LE directors made him a "general manager" on the spot. He then retreated back into the station to ponder his new-found authority. Eventually the TH and B assumed the line and operated under the CPR until the 1980s.

Not all station agents were full time. Many were simply caretakers. Their job was to open or close the station, set the fires in the waiting room stove, and handle the freight and mail. They could not, however, ticket passengers or relay train orders. In 1910 the Board of Railway Commissioners, which oversaw all railway matters, decreed that any station with earnings less than fifteen thousand dollars a year did not require an agent. While this forced the railways to hire operator agents at some previously unmanned locations where earnings exceeded fifteen thousand dollars annually, it also meant that they could demote some full-time agents to caretaker agents at others.

The duties of the caretaker agent were, according to a later CN staff bulletin, "to see that the station building was kept clean, heated, and lighted for the accommodation of the passengers, and to take care of LCL [less than carload] freight shipments." Originally, the order stipulated that caretaker agents could not sell tickets. However, the howl from the railways and passengers was so great that the commissioners routinely exempted caretakers from that prohibition.

The decline in revenue during the Depression heralded a flood of requests from the railways asking the Board to downgrade agents to caretaker agents. Within two years, more than 400 agents were downgraded to caretakers. Clearly, the demotions were a hardship, for salaries tumbled too. To alleviate the problem, the railways often allowed the former agents to continue to inhabit the station and paid them higher wages than those they paid to newly-hired caretaker agents. In addition, the railways allowed them to continue to earn commissions on telegraph, express, and ticket sales.

The Kingston and Pembroke line north of Kingston, Ontario, was a case in point. After the CPR purchased the line, it demoted many of the operators to caretakers. Hilda Geddes's father became caretaker of the Snow Road,

The interior of Bellis Station, now located in the Ukrainian Heritage Park east of Edmonton, Alberta.

to be phoned to the operator at the Lavant station twelve miles away.

After the World War II, life for full agents became a little easier. On September 1, 1949, agents in the U.S. finally obtained what other workers already took for granted: the 40-hour week. Almost two years later, after heavy bargaining between the Order of Railroad Telegraphers and the management of CN and CP, Canadian agents received the same. At the same time agents became entitled to two consecutive days off per week, one of which had to be a Sunday. Suddenly dozens of communities all across Canada found their beloved agents weren't so beloved any more. Station doors that had been open evenings and weekends were locked; the agents stubbornly refusing to open them. Letters and telegrams flooded the Board of Transport Commissioners, warning of industrial or economic collapse within many small communities.

Ontario, station. Although the station had been an operator station before the CPR take-over, and retained the operator's bay window and ticket office, Geddes's father conducted the railway's business from his general store, Hilda Geddes's home to this day.

Clyde Forks was another K and P caretaker station. Here a renovated boxcar served as waiting room and freight shed. According to Mel Easton, K and P historian, the caretaker was an elderly lady named Sarah who lived in the village a mile away. At train time the villagers would "wheel" her on the freight wagon down to the station, where she would light the stove and check for freight. Because the station had no telegraph, notice of freight shipments, usually wood from the mill, had

At Home in the Station

Although it is now a way of life that is almost forgotten, many Canadians were born in, got married in, lived in, and died in railway stations. To attract steady and reliable family men into agent positions, the railways incorporated into many of their station plans accommodation for the agent and his family, typically a large second storey on the building. Through the back door of his office, the agent could quickly retreat to his combined dining/living room. The kitchen was located beside the back door, while three or sometimes four bedrooms would be situated upstairs. This was usually necessary in new or remote communities, where housing was scarce.

Station agents didn't usually consider their jobs particularly dangerous. This collision at Collins Bay station near Kingston, (Known locally as the"Sheep wreck") must have had the agent thinking twice.

The Grand Trunk Railway, on the other hand, passed very close to established towns and cities, and live-in quarters were not necessary. The GTR generally preferred to provide a separate house. Some GTR station plans, however, especially those for remoter locations or smaller communities, contained upstairs living quarters. In 1923, after the CNR had assumed the Grand Trunk's assets, most of the agents' houses were sold or demolished. But along the former Canadian Northern lines the CNR did continue to construct stations to original CNo plans, complete with comfortable quarters upstairs.

Although by today's standards living conditions were difficult, by the standards of the day they were better than most. Ed Holmes recalls his life at the station in Keewatin, Ontario: "Our living quarters were heated by two stoves...a big coal and wood range in the kitchen and a 'self feeding' heater in the living room. The upstairs bedrooms went unheated, absorbing what heat came from the pipes that lead from the downstairs to the roof, or through vents in the floor. Coal was supplied free by the railways."

Amenities that we take for granted were slow and inconsistent in arriving. Ray Gilchrist, now of Lethbridge, Alberta, had electricity at his station as early as 1922, while

Bernice Sanderson of Avonlea, Saskatchewan, didn't have indoor plumbing until the 1960s. Some couldn't wait that long. "I remember my mother telling me a story," reminisces F.A. Howard-Gibbon in *The Coupler* . "She wasn't too keen about moving into [the] Williams Lake [station]. Especially when she discovered the privy for the railway station outside down beside the tracks. It was one of those bisexual jobs. One side for the ladies and one side for the gents. It was for the patrons of the railroad, and incidentally to serve for the station agent and his family. 'I don't want to have to go downstairs and across the yard all winter long to go to the bathroom,' she complained. So they put a bathroom in."

Often the agents' families simply outgrew the crowded quarters. When the family of the caretaker agent at St Lazare, Quebec, began expanding, the CPR simply severed off a piece of the waiting room to create a third bedroom. By his retirement in 1942 the family numbered eight; and the station had been significantly enlarged.

Despite living within meters of thundering freight trains, those who lived in stations did not see station life as a dangerous existence. It was not, however, without some risks. In the days of wood-burning locomotives a stray ember might land in the woodpile and ignite a blaze that could quickly engulf the station. Indeed, one early station burned down the day it opened. Faulty wheels or twisted tracks occasionally launched a train into the side of the station. The agent at Franz, Ontario, barely escaped when train ploughed into his office. The little wooden CPR station at Rogers Pass, B.C., was nestled below the snow-covered peaks of the mountains; in January

1899 the snow suddenly shook loose, roared down the mountain side, and smashed into the station. The agent and his young family were killed instantly; only the servant girl survived.

Trying to sleep literally ten feet from a busy railway track was not for insomniacs. Trains that rumbled through, often several times a night, set dishes rattling and plaster falling. Should a road crossing be located nearby—and there usually was—the deafening blast from the engine's whistle would roar through the bedroom windows.

Winter brought its own problems. No sooner would an agent sweep the platform following a heavy storm, than the plough train would dump the snow right back onto the platform—sometimes sending chunks of frozen snow crashing through the office or waiting room windows.

During the 1920s and 1930s the railways tried to make station life easier. To alleviate the bitter winter cold and reduce maintenance costs, the railways added insulation; for the CPR it was insulbrick, for the CNR stucco. Then came electricity, generally in the 1920s, and finally indoor plumbing. The latter was usually the last amenity, with some station agents relying on the outdoor privy until well into the 1960s.

For kids such as Ed Holmes, the station presented unusual opportunities for play, play that might worry most parents. "Growing up in Keewatin's station poses grave concerns for one's parents in particular; with Portage Bay and a lot of water on one side and a very busy railway right-of-way on the other side, my mother must have spent the greater part of each day running back and forth from one window to another to make

Station agents' families often helped in almost every aspect of the work.

sure we hadn't drowned or been run over by a train."

Games, however, were unlike those of any other youngsters. "A friend of mine and I were walking on top of a number of cook cars on a siding east of the station," recalls Holmes. "We happened to look down a ventilator on one of the cars and there below on a stove was a pot of prunes [also called CPR strawberries] boiling away. We gathered up a number of clean white egg-sized stones from the roadbed ballast and dropped them unnoticed through the ventilator into the pot below. We didn't wait around for the gang when they returned to the cook cars for supper."

Helena Campbell, now of Simcoe, Ontario, recalls that in her station home at Wellwood, Manitoba, "five days of the week when no trains passed through, we children and our playmates utilized the station areas, the waiting room, the freight sheds and the extensive platform. All the children in town played with us there."

For families in isolated stations, life was probably not unlike that experienced by Alice Takacs during her childhood in a section house near Manyberries, Alberta. "We lived in wilderness and isolation. Our friends were the gophers, antelope and rattlesnakes. Evenings were special. Our family would gather around the Marconi and listen to our favourite programs, Lux Radio Theatre, John and Judy, and Wayne and Schuster.... At ten in the morning everything would stop for the Happy Gang."

As with the station agents, the railway supplied most of the family's needs. "Every other Monday the train would bring us our water supply for two weeks, placed in a cis-

tern," adds Takacs. "On Tuesdays in a specially made wooden box two quarts of milk would arrive from Manyberries.... In the dirt basement we would store our canned food stuffs. In quart sealers we would have such items as beef, pork, peas, carrots, beans and pickles."

Well-provisioned or not, it was always a relief to get away. "Fridays were always the highlight of the week. This was the day we would get ready to go into Manyberries by train to pick up our mail and do grocery shopping."

Living as they did in the station building, families became part of station operations. Helena Campbell relates: "Mother had learned telegraphy too...as a child we were all taught the call for Wellwood so we could alert Daddy, who might be in the garden, that he was wanted on the wire. Daddy also rigged up a telegraph line between the office and the living quarters. Mother used to call him to meals or tell him that so and so was heading for the station (she had a view of the town from the living room area)."

This familiarity often meant that generations of families became railway families. Clayton Cook's three sisters received work with the Newfoundland Railway and Telegraph and with the Canadian National Telegraphs, all because they had learned telegraphy while living in a station. As a child, Ray Gilchrist of Lethbridge earned five dollars a month from the CPR for cleaning the chimneys of his father's station and filling the semaphore lamps once a month.

Many marriages vows were exchanged in stations. The terminal supervisor in a CPR divisional station in northern Ontario met his future wife while she was working in the

Many marriage vows were exchanged in stations; here a wedding party leaves the station at Sandon, British Columbia in 1904.

The residents of this remote station and community at Metagama in northern Ontario formed an arts and letters society to forget their isolation.

restaurant of another divisional station. Ed Holmes' wife, Nonie, assembled her bridal bouquet from the flowers that were growing in the Keewatin station garden, while both Helena Campbell and her sister were married in the large CPR station at Virden.

Living in a station was not always easy. "Cooking was a bit of a problem," recalls Donald Leslie. "A general store in Nelson made up a parcel for me every week with sugar, pepper, salt, butter, bacon, bread, potatoes, tea, eggs, and condensed milk...those were the days before refrigeration other than the old ice box, and I had none.... I built a meat safe arrangement with fly-screen sides which I kept in the creek under the railway

bridge.... The earth oven was really a five-gallon coal oil can on its side with space for a fire underneath it.... It took me a little time to get onto controlling the heat, but after a while a roast could be cooked deliciously."

While most station accommodations were substantial, some stations were little more than shacks. Donald Leslie describes his station at Troup Junction as "perhaps six by ten with a partition dividing off the one bunk bedroom from the 'office,' which held a small kitchen table, a caboose pot-bellied mushroom-topped coal stove and a shelf table for the telegraph instruments and train register, and I think that was all."

Another problem was isolation, which struck agents in northern Ontario the worst. With no farmland around, the many stations attracted neither settlers nor villagers. They remained isolated in a silent forest, an existence made tolerable only by the arrival of trains, communication with other agents, or the visits of the dental or school cars. The few residents of the isolated community of Metagama in northern Ontario formed an arts and letters society and endured the long and lonely isolation by organizing concerts and carnivals.

The years that followed the Second World War changed forever the role that the station agents played in Canada's communities. TVs and telephones replaced the agent's telegraph key as the link with the outside world. Residents of Canada's small communities began to see less and less of their agent.

Then in the 1950s, after a hard battle, railway employees finally achieved what most other Canadians had been enjoying for decades: the forty-hour work week. Suddenly station hours were like those of any other business: the doors closed at 5. (When longer hours were required substitute agents manned the building.) One result was that the station lost its role as a community drop-in centre. By 1960 the agent was no longer a key member of the community, but had become just another railway employee.

By the early 1970s the agents had ceased to handle local freight and mail, their role reduced to train inspection and train order handling. A few continued to live in the stations, but most lived out, for the buildings had become outdated and difficult to heat. Maintenance slipped, and many became fire traps, expensive to insure.

By the end of the 1970s, with traffic d control centralized, station agents had become redundant and thousands were given their notice. While most agents retired, many were given jobs as dispatchers in the large central offices or as terminal supervisors at divisional stations. A few agents remained in local stations to handle specialized tasks. An operator remained in the Medonte, Ontario, station as late as 1991 to operate the signals at a diamond. But such jobs were few and soon vanished altogether. Even the term "agent" has been dropped from the railway lexicon.

There are still operators and dispatchers, there are still switchers, roadmasters and engineers, and section foremen, but the railway station agent has, like the steam engines and the stations, become just a memory.

(above) A scene on the Port Arthur, Duluth and Western Railway (now known as the "ghost railway to nowhere") near Thunder Bay.

(opposite) Children at play, Grandes Piles station, Quebec.

The Station as a Place to Play

For many Canadians their small-town station was a place to travel, to socialize, or to work. It symbolized their town and was their gateway to the outside. But for other Canadians the station was a focus for recreation, a place to play.

By the 1850s the Industrial Revolution had swept England's small towns, overwhelming them with its smoke and its row housing and thrusting upon the workers long unrewarding hours in dreadful factories or mines. Many tried to blot out their environment by maintaining an alcoholic stupor. Thomas Cook, a temperance advocate, took one of the Industrial Revolution's own inventions to provide an alternative to booze. That invention was the railway. In the 1850s he began organizing Sunday rail excursions for city workers. These outings, usually to the sea, proved an enormous success and launched Thomas Cook into the travel industry, where his name remains over a century later.

Ontario's first railway, the Erie and Ontario, entered the tourist business early. Originally a horse-drawn portage railway between Chippawa and Queenston, the line was soon extended to Niagara-on-the-Lake and Fort Erie. In 1855 the line published ads that claimed it had the most attractive tourist route "in North America." It connected with steamers to Toronto and offered onward connections via the Ontario Simcoe and Huron railway to steamers between Collingwood and Sault Ste Marie, or Lake Superior.

Most Canadians, however, preferred local excursions. From its very sighting by Samuel de Champlain, the foaming cataract at Niagara Falls was a popular excursion destina-

The wharfside Great Western (later Grand Trunk) station at Port Dalhousie
on Lake Ontario, with the 'Empress of India' moored at the adjacent dock.

tion. "There is but one Niagara Falls on earth
and but one great railway to it," boasted the
Michigan Central Railway, which had acquired the Erie and Ontario. By the brink of
the falls it built the six-sided Falls View Station, designed to resemble a summerhouse,
and landscaped it with a lawn and flowers.
As the railway literature vaunted, "Falls View
[Station],...as the name indicates, is a splen-
did point from which to view the great cataract...thousands of beauty lovers and
grandeur worshippers will journey over the
only railway from which it can be seen." The
Michigan Central added two other tourist stations, at Clifton Hill and Wesley Park, both
now part of the town of Niagara Falls.

Ontario's many lakeside stations became
popular for Sunday school picnics. The Great
Western station at Port Dalhousie was one.
"We arrived at the [station] ground in some-

what of a jam," recalls one reveller, "one loco
brought down the cars filled within and on
top, water was in great demand...a great
many baskets were very quickly emptied of
their contents...to the great comfort of all." In
1901 the Niagara, St. Catharines and Toronto
Electric Railway added not only a station at
Port Dalhousie but an amusement park as
well. Steamers brought excursionists across
the lake from Toronto to the popular little station.

In 1876 the Hamilton and Northwestern
Railway built a line on the beach that divided
Lake Ontario from Burlington Bay, and built
a station that became one of the area's most
popular excursion destinations. Close and
cheap, Hamilton Beach attracted steel-plant
workers from their hot and smoky refineries.
They tumbled from the trains and into such
beachside taverns as well as the Wells, the

Sportsmans Arms, the Grey House, and Dynes
Hotel. Others built small cottages. Although
the station has been demolished after serving
many years as a private home, the tracks
have been lifted, and most of the hotels replaced, the Dynes Hotel remains a popular
local cocktail lounge, while the cottages have
been converted to permanent homes.

North of Toronto, the sandy beaches and
clear waters of Lake Simcoe drew sweating
city dwellers to stations at Keswick, Jacksons
Point, or Sutton on the Toronto and
York Radial line, or to stations
like Port Bolster or Maple
Beach.

One of the most popular of Canada's excursion stations was that at Port Stanley, Ontario. Ever since the London and Port Stanley
line opened in 1853, it had been popular
with landlocked Londoners seeking waterside
escape that was close and cheap. Port Stanley
was less than a hour away. Although the line
was originally opened to haul farm products
and lumber to the port and bring coal back
up to London, it had by 1915 carried over
twenty-eight million passengers to the beach.
Later, as the big-band era swept the continent, evening excursions were added; aficio-
nados flocked to hear the bands play at Port
Stanley's Stork Club while the reflection of
the hazy summer moon shimmered in Erie's
waters.

Although the line was short, it proved so
popular that the Michigan Central, which operated it for a time, added an attractive red
sandstone station downtown opposite that of
the GTR.

By 1957 Londoners had turned to cars to
carry them to other beaches, and passenger
service on the London and Port Stanley

The Mount Stephen House station/hotel at Field, British Columbia, was Van Horne's first attempt to use the breathtaking scenery through with the CPR passed to develop that railway's tourist business.

Metropolitan Toronto Reference Library

ended. But unlike other railway lines that died and disappeared, the LPS has revived. Thanks to Brad Jodliffe and Al Howlett, the line once again transports tourists. Although the London station has long been demolished, excursions run between the Port Stanley station and the tiny shelter at Union.

Excursion stations were not peculiar to Ontario. Victoria Beach, a Canadian Northern station on Lake Winnipegosis, gave Winnipegers much-needed relief from the hot, dry prairie summers. Vancouver Islanders climbed onto the coaches of the Esquimalt and Nanaimo Railway to visit seaside stations at Nanaimo or Qualicum. Goldstream Station near Victoria attracted excursionists who crowded the station grounds to hear Victoria's Fifth Regiment band fill the summer air with brassy military marches.

The CPR and the Hotel Era

"If we can't export the scenery we'll import the tourists," thundered William Cornelius Van Horne. As the CPR's vice president in 1884, he was in charge of scenery. A capitalist in the American tradition, Van Horne was fully prepared to turn the overwhelming scenery that the CPR passed through into tourist dollars. Van Horne's perception and initiative led to Canada's greatest hotel-building era (true hotels, not the prefabricated look-alikes that dominate our highways today).

Like the CPR's first stations, its first hotels were born of necessity, were simple in appearance, and had little to do with scenery. Because the railway dining cars were too heavy for CPR's engines to haul through the mountains, they were left behind. In their place, to

provide for the hungry and well-heeled diner, the CPR built a string of station-hotels.

The first of these were the Mount Stephen House at Field, the Glacier House at Rogers Pass, and the Fraser Canyon House at North Bend, all similar in layout and designed by Thomas Sorby. A fourth was built in Revelstoke. Although the stations were intended to be restaurants with a few rooms added on, Van Horne discovered that the tourists were staying on to enjoy the scenery before proceeding.

Van Horne then hired the world's best architects to build more and better hotels. Working in the chateauesque style, which set Canada apart in the world of station architecture, Bruce Price, Edward Maxwell, and Frances Rattenbury added the Empress Hotel at Victoria, the Hotel Vancouver in Vancouver,

CP Corporate Archives A 1679

The mountains tower high above the CPR's popular Glacier House hotel and station.

the Banff Springs and the Chateau Lake Louise in the Rocky Mountains, the Palliser in Calgary, the Royal Alexandra in Winnipeg, and the Chateau Montebello and Chateau Frontenac in Quebec.

What might have been Canada's first station-hotel was never built. In 1880, with the CPR's transcontinental line on hold, the railway chose a remote lumber town named Algoma Mills on the Sault Ste Marie line as a steamer terminus. To take full advantage of Lake Huron's north-shore scenery Van Horne hired architect Thomas Sorby to design what would have been CPR's first recreational hotel. Although the foundation was laid, the two-storey hotel was never built, for John A. MacDonald's Tories were re-elected and revived the transcontinental route. The Sault line was downgraded to branch status, and Algoma Mills became just another wayside station.

But it was the new combination station-hotels that set the CPR's facilities apart in the railway recreation business. The station-hotels at Rogers Pass, Field, and North Bend were enlarged, while others were added in British Columbia at Cameron Lake and Strathcona on Vancouver Island, at Belfour and Sicamous in southern B.C., and still others were built at Medicine Hat, Moose Jaw, Montreal (Viger), and Macadam, New Brunswick. Built in the imposing chateauesque style, these buildings incorporated rooms upstairs and elegant (and expensive) dining rooms at ground level as well as waiting rooms and facilities for the agent.

By 1890 the CPR was well into the tourist business and was promoting the mountains of Alberta and B.C. as the Canadian Alps. Of all the mountain stations, Glacier House became the most popular. Initially built as a dining room, the Glacier House had a mere six rooms for overnight accommodation. But looming high above the little hotel was the mighty Illecillewaet Glacier that, as one visitor put it, "pours seemingly out of the sky in a magnificent ice cascade and descends into the valley towards the hotel as a massive fissured tongue."

No wonder that in a day when wealthy Victorian tourists were taking to nature, space at the Glacier House was quickly in high demand. In 1892 the CPR added a thirty-two-bedroom annex, and in 1906 a second with more than fifty. With its glacier, its mountain climbing, and its meals, Glacier House had become one of Canada's premier tourist attractions. Unlike at other station-hotels, Glacier House's station was not in the hotel as such, but rather was a small log shelter located a few metres away.

Just as the snowcapped mountains had brought about the success of Glacier House, the mountains destroyed it, for that area of the Rogers Pass was the worst avalanche area in the mountains. When in 1910 the same peaks unleashed a torrent of billowing snow upon sixty-two hapless CPR crewmen, the CPR chose to head under the mountains and bypass the side valley where the Glacier House stood. In 1916 CPR engineers finished the famous Connaught Tunnel, the world's longest double-track tunnel.

Glacier House was suddenly no longer accessible by train. Although visitors now had to reach the hotel by buggy, it remained open for another ten years. In 1926 the CPR closed the hotel forever, and in 1929 demolished it.

On the opposite side of the continent stood another of the CPR's great station-ho-

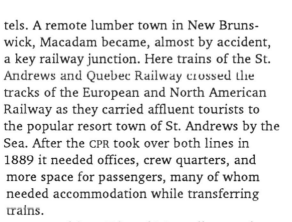

Tourists travelling the CPR to St. Andrew's "by the sea" in New Brunswick looked forward to staying in the Macadam station/hotel.

The CPR's Sicamous station/hotel (seen here ca. 1900) was squeezed between the CP main line and the lake waters.

tels. A remote lumber town in New Brunswick, Macadam became, almost by accident, a key railway junction. Here trains of the St. Andrews and Quebec Railway crossed the tracks of the European and North American Railway as they carried affluent tourists to the popular resort town of St. Andrews by the Sea. After the CPR took over both lines in 1889 it needed offices, crew quarters, and more space for passengers, many of whom needed accommodation while transferring trains.

CPR architect Edward Maxwell created a massive stone station-hotel in the CPR's now trademark "chateau" style that, while in keeping with the railway's tourist image (it was nearly identical to his other station-hotels at Moose Jaw and Medicine Hat), was out of all proportion to the tiny lumber town. It did, however, help lure tourists to the CPR's Algon-

quin Hotel in nearby St. Andrews. On the main floor travellers could snack at a lunch counter or dine at linen-covered tables in the dining room. On the second floor they could settle into one of seventeen comfortable rooms while awaiting overnight train connections. On the third floor twenty-eight young women, employees of the hotel and dining room, crowded into their tiny staff quarters, subject to a rigid 10 p.m. curfew.

In the 1960s the hotel was closed to commercial patrons. Trains declined from sixteen a day to less than ten a week, while yard staff dwindled from 650 to just 35.

Bruce Price's trademark chateau style also appeared in Edward Maxwell's station-hotels at Moose Jaw and Medicine Hat, which, like that at Macadam, were primarily layover stations.

The Sicamous station-hotel was squeezed between the CPR main line and the waters of

Lake Okanagan. Designed by Maxwell, it was built in 1897. An addition in 1910 that nearly doubled the size of the building obliterated most of its chateau turrets and roofline. It was finally demolished in the early 1960s.

The CPR's other station-hotels suffered various fates. The Glacier House was demolished in 1929, the Field House became a YMCA and survived until the 1950s, and the station at Moose Jaw was replaced by a larger office and waiting room in 1922. But three of the most magnificent have survived. That at Medicine Hat continues to provide divisional office space for the CPR; in Montreal the Viger Hotel was converted into municipal offices; and the stone station-hotel at Macadam, New Brunswick, now designated as a national historic monument, continues to serve as a divisional point.

A popular spot for Vancouver Islanders was the CPR's Strathcona Station/Hotel. Designed by a Victoria architect named McLure, the Strathcona Hotel was operated by the Shawinigan Lake Hotel Group until it was taken over by the CPR in 1916. The CPR added station facilities and operated it as a station-hotel until 1927, when it was sold to a private girls' school. Its thirty-two rooms, its fifty acres of landscaped lakeside lawns, and its croquet and tennis facilities made it one of the most popular destinations for west-coast holidayers. The building continued to function as a combined station and girls' school until it was finally demolished in 1969.

CP Corporate Archives A 19542

Log Stations

The rustic appeal of log construction has long been a tourist lure. With the trend to nature vacations in the 1890s, log stations became part of the railways' efforts to attract visitors to their lines and their hotels. As William Van Horne advised his station builders, "Lots of good logs there. Cut them, peel them and build your station." Where the railway line was close to the hotel, the station facilities were in the hotel itself, or in a small nearby structure. If the hotel was some distance away and out of sight, the railways wanted to ensure that the first thing a disembarking passenger saw had high visual appeal, and that was usually the station.

When the loop line to Glacier House was replaced by the more distance Cannaught tunnel, the station that was opened to serve the hotel was constructed of logs and was named "Glacier." Similarly, the CPR erected log stations to serve their hotels at Banff and Lake Louise. While that at Banff was replaced by an equally appealing frame station, that at Lake Louise was replaced by another log structure. The original log station (named Laggan) now rests in Calgary's Heritage Park; its replacement still stands.

Ontario and Quebec, with their lake-studded vacation lands accessible at first only by train, also claimed a large number of log stations. Two of the best known were the Joe Lake station built along the Grand Trunk line in Algonquin Park to serve the Algonquin Hotel, and the now-relocated Montebello station built east of Ottawa to serve the CPR's magnificent and still functioning Chateau

Montebello.

Canada's most northerly log station was that of the White Pass and Yukon Route in Whitehorse, N.W.T. As part of a community revitalization effort, log siding was added in the 1950s to a station that replaced the original, which had burned in 1905.

Although log stations had the most appeal, other station-hotels used standard patterns; such as that erected by the Grand Trunk for its Highland Inn in Algonquin Park. The National Transcontinental station built at Minaki for the Minaki Lodge followed a pattern found in seven other NT stations in northwestern Ontario. Only that at Minaki survives, and is today a gift shop.

Steamer Stations

Steamer stations were special lakeside stations where travellers could transfer quickly from train to steamer. In Ontario, a string of large lakes, known as the Muskokas, lay temptingly close to Toronto and other growing cities. Their (then) clear waters, their (then) peaceful bays, and their (then) tree-lined shores all appealed to city dwellers tired of the noise, the crowd, and the smell of nineteenth-century urban Canada.

As early as the 1870s the trains of the Northern Railway began hauling the wealthier tourists to the lakes. At such lakeside towns as Gravenhurst, Huntsville, and Burks Falls the Northern constructed sidings to the steamer wharves, where a fleet of steamers waited to carry the happy throngs off to the several hotels that in the pre-cottage era offered the only comfortable form of lakeside vacation.

When the Grand Trunk took over the Northern Railway, and when the CPR and the Canadian Northern built new lines along the west side of the Muskoka lakes, more steamer stations quickly appeared. The Canadian Northern constructed steamer stations at Bala Park and Torrance on Lake Muskoka and at Barnesdale on Lake Joseph, while the CPR also added structures at Bala and Barnesdale.

Most steamer stations were little more than shelters. A small enclosed area provided an office for the operator and foul-weather waiting space for passengers. For the most part, however, steamer stations were distinguished by their large, canopied, open waiting areas. Only that at Muskoka Wharf in Gravenhurst, designed by Grand Trunk architect Joseph Hobson, could claim to be of any size or to have architectural embellishment.

Because the steamer stations were seasonal, the railway often had a second, winter station at such locations. In addition to its station at Muskoka Wharf, Gravenhurst had a year-round station on the main line east of the town. The CNo had separate winter stations at Barnesdale and Bala Park, while the CPR had a winter station, in its standard style, at Bala. Burks Falls, like Gravenhurst had a large two-storey pattern-book station on the main line, while a small plain steamer station huddled by the Magnetawan River. At Huntsville the main-line station stood just across the track from the steamer station. Steamers with names like the Armour, the Sagamo, or the Seguin would depart the wharf stations after meeting the train from Toronto, and puff off, their decks jammed with bags and crates and alive with milling passengers, destined for camps, cottages, and hotels.

The log exterior was added to Canada's most northerly station at Whitehorse, Northwest Territories in the 1950s to help the community's tourist image.

Montebello, Quebec.

141

CP Archives

A Lake Joseph steamer awaits train passengers at the Lake Joseph steamer station.

The whimsical Muskoka Wharf station at Gravenhurst was home to the Muskoka Lakes steamer fleet.

Metropoloitan Toronto Reference Library

Muskoka's steamer stations were vital for the area's permanent settlements as well, many just barely out of the pioneer stages. Villages like Rosseau, Port Carling, and Port Sandfield on the Muskoka lakes or Cecebe, Magnetawan, and Ahmic Harbour on the Magnetawan River all depended upon the steamers for groceries, hardware, and supplies.

Following the First World War, trains of the CPR and the new CNR began to make fewer and fewer calls at the steamer stations, preferring the cheaper alternative of dropping passengers at the main-line stations. More and more people were buying cars and cottages and following the crude roads that led to them. The popularity of the grand hotels and the steamers declined drastically.

The years that followed the Second World War saw the steamer stations disappear completely. Cottage fever swept Ontario, roads were paved, and suddenly everyone owned a car. Cottage-bound urbanites were prepared to endure five-hour traffic jams in return for the flexibility of driving their own car to their own cottage.

In 1954 the CNR, which had been collecting one thousand dollars a year from the navigation companies for use of its Muskoka Wharf station, shut down the station completely. In 1959 the building was demolished. The steamer era in the Muskokas had ended, and with it went the once-busy steamer stations. Although a restored Seguin once again puffs around the Muskoka lakes, reliving the steamers' glory days, the stations are gone for good.

Railway steamer stations also appeared at many Canadian ports. But they were not just for tourists; they were fundamental to

Canada's transportation system. One of the first important Great Lakes steamer stations was that built at Collingwood on the Northern Railway in 1854, an attractive station with a tower, landscaped with gardens and offering music from its bandshell. The Northern Railway provided steamer connections from its station at Belle Ewart to the Lake Simcoe ports of Barrie, Orillia, Beaverton, and Sutton, and to the railway's popular Couchiching Hotel.

In 1874 the Whitby and Port Perry Extension Railway provided steamer service from its wharf station in Port Perry to Lindsay. Service ended just three years later when the railway line itself reached Lindsay. At Deseronto, Ontario, a combination warehouse and station linked the trains of the Napanee, Tamworth and Quebec (later the Bay of Quinte) Railway to the New York state ports of Oswego and Sodus Point.

One of Ontario's oldest stations was that built by the Grand Trunk Railway at Kingston, Ontario. In 1860 the GTR extended a branch from the main-line "outer station" into downtown Kingston and built a brick, mansard-roofed station to provide travellers with steamer connections to New York state. Although now surrounded by high-rise apartments, the station still stands, its facade little altered in over 130 years.

At Owen Sound on Georgian Bay a pair of steamer stations stared across the harbour at each other until 1912, when the CPR moved its steamer operation further east to Port McNicoll. The new port quickly became the busiest on the lakes, transferring coachloads of tourists as well as hopperloads of grain to and from CP's Great Lakes steamers.

Other Great Lakes wharf stations included

those on the St. Lawrence River at Brockville and Prescott, that of the Thousand Islands Railway in Gananoque, the Michigan Central's at Niagara-on-the-Lake, and those on Lake Erie at Port Dover and Port Burwell. Toronto, despite its importance as both a railway centre and a port, never had a steamer station.

Following World War Two the increased use of trucks and larger trains eliminated many wharfside stations. The last of the CPR's fleet of Great Lakes steamers puffed out of Port McNicoll in 1963. The era of the steamer station was over.

Although scant evidence remains of most steamer stations, a few have survived. The CPR summer station at French River near Sudbury was moved to a nearby lot, and the TIR

A CP steamship glides to the dock and an awaiting train at the Port McNicoll station, a popular transfer spot for tourists and Great Lakes steamship passengers.

This pattern book Grand Trunk station in Ontario's Algonquin Park was familiar to many wilderness seekers. The anxieties of tourists apprehensive at staying in rooms that overlooked a noisy and smoky railway track were allayed by the rules at Algonquin Park Station, which prohibited switching at night and blowing the whistle near the hotel, and which ordered engineers to shut off steam when passing.

station at Gananoque remained on site as a gift shop and restaurant; it burned in 1991. At Owen Sound two stations still stare across the harbour at each other. That of the CNR now belongs to a community group, while that of the CPR, a "new era"–style structure that never saw steamer service, remains a CP terminal.

Canada's other major lake-studded playground was the Kootenay area of southern British Columbia. At the beginning, however, recreation was minimal. The lodes of gold, silver, copper, and coal attracted a half dozen railway lines, all requiring steamer stations.

Eventually the CPR and the Great Northern acquired the smaller lines, and both maintained steamer fleets. The CPR continued passenger service on the lakes until 1957 and barge service for a further two decades.

Most stations conformed to standard plans. Survivors include the GN's small station-hotel at Kuskonoosh and the CPR's station at Kaslo. Both lines have been long abandoned. The former CP steamer *Moyie* has survived, drawn onto the shore and converted into a museum.

Algonquin Park

While the CPR was touting the Rocky Mountains as Canada's great natural resource, the GTR had a natural treasure of its own, Ontario's Algonquin Park.

In 1893 the area became a provincial park. Although long promoted for its "wilderness," seventy-five per cent of the park was actually set aside for logging, a role that it retains to this day, Nevertheless, its tourist allure was strong and did not escape the owners of the railway.

In 1904 the GTR acquired from John Rudolphus Booth the Canada Atlantic Railway. The CAR had in part served as Booth's logging railway between Ottawa and Parry Sound, built not only to haul lumber from Algonquin Park but to ship grain from the West to the Atlantic.

The GTR wasted little time in going after tourists. In 1908 it built the Highland Inn Hotel in the middle of the park. Hugely popular, the hotel was expanded to seventy-five guestrooms in 1913. Just steps from its front door the GTR placed one of its own stations, built in a style common in southwestern Ontario.

West of the Highland Inn the line swung north to hug the shores of Joe Lake. Here the railway built another hotel, the Hotel Algonquin. To complement the wilderness theme that the railway was trying to sell, the engineers designed the station of logs.

The GTR heavily promoted its recreational experience. It placed pictures of Algonquin Park on playing cards and offered packaged wilderness canoe excursions that originated at Canoe Lake Station, included overnight stays at the Nominigan Lodge, and ended at the Highland Inn itself.

Algonquin Park was not the only opportunity to enjoy nature on this GTR line. West of Parry Sound tourists disembarked at the twin-towered Rose Point Station and crossed the small bay to the Rose Point Hotel. Travellers from Buffalo took the "Buffalo Flyer" to the Maple Lake Hotel located near Swords.

The 1930s marked the decline of the recreational stations in Algonquin Park. In that decade the government of Canada responded to the crushing unemployment of the depression by initiating a road-building program, one that included extending roads into Algonquin Park. Then in 1933 a railway bridge east of the Highland Inn was damaged. Rather than repair the bridge, the CNR, since 1923 the owner of the GTR, simply cut off through service.

Nevertheless, recreational trains continued to rumble into the Algonquin Park station until the late 1950s. But by then cottages had replaced hotels as the preferred summer recreational form, and the private auto had replaced the passenger train as the way to get there. There was, after all, no other way to travel to private cottages.

Ontario Archives Acc 9912-1-7

Unable to compete with the cottage and the car, the Highland Inn was demolished and the Nomingan was sold. (The Algonquin had burned some years earlier.) The stations were ripped out and the tracks torn up.

The shortsighted love affair with the car is regretted to this day by harried wilderness seekers who must now endure mind-numbing traffic jams, and by families with young children who would prefer to see Algonquin Park from the comfort of a lodge rather than from remote and rocky campsites.

The Campers' Specials

Although eastern Canada is perceived as the urban and agricultural heartland of Canada, much of it has remained undeveloped, primar-

Happy hunters pose proudly with their prey of deer, moose and skunk on the platform of Haliburton's original Grand Trunk station.

Fishers share their catch with the train crew beside this private resort station in northern Ontario.

ily in the rocky, lake-strewn reaches of northern Ontario and Quebec. From the early days of railway travel these remote regions attracted fishermen, canoeists, and cottagers, or "campers," as they are called in these areas.

"Cacoma is a quiet enough way station during the greater part of the year," noted one travel writer in the 1920s, "but during July and August it is one of the busiest on the line. Big trunks line the platform and crowded omnibuses fly to and fro...boats dance upon the water while the gay and festive dance upon the land...in the winter it subsides into an ordinary village, empty houses abound, the great hotel is abandoned to darkness."

During the 1920s recreation began to play a greater role in the lives of Canadians. The two-week vacation, unheard of before the First World War, became a common part of the year's routine. Wherever railway lines twisted through the romantic wilds of northern Ontario and Quebec, tourists followed. Fishing and hunting camps began to appear along the routes of the former National Transcontinental west of Nakina, along the route of the CPR between Sudbury and White River, along the route of the Algoma Central Railway north of Sault Ste Marie, and along the CNR between Shawinigan and Jonquiere in Quebec.

Special trains were put on just to transport the tourists. One of the more famous and enduring was the "Campers' Special." Departing Winnipeg each sultry summer Friday evening, it carried eager cottagers to the shores of Malachi, Ottermere, and Farlane lakes in northwestern Ontario. Many were employees of the CNR who had received their cottage lots directly from the railway. The cot-

tages remain accessible only by train to this day. However, in 1990 the federal government forced Via Rail to reroute Canada's only remaining transcontinental train, the "Canadian," from CPR to CNR trackage (trackage that, according to a CN employee, will itself be lifted by 1996 and leave the "Canadian" with nowhere to go) and to replace the Campers' Special with a less convenient schedule that no longer permits the cottagers Friday–Sunday round trips.

The stations that serve the cottagers vary in style. In northwestern Ontario, those at Farlane and Malachi are former operator stations designed by the CNR in the 1920s largely for northwestern Ontario locations, while those at Ottermere and Wade, dating from the same period, are simpler flag stations with no accommodation for operators. Although no longer used by the railway most are carefully maintained by the cottagers.

For the campers and natives along the ACR line north of Sault Ste Marie umbrella stations provide shelter, while elsewhere in northern Ontario along the CN and CP lines passengers are unloaded onto bare and grassy trackside meadows with only a signpost to mark the location.

Newfoundlanders were not even that lucky. On October 28, 1989, the last passenger train of the Newfoundland Railway (CNR) departed Bishops Falls for Corner Brook. Although townspeople along the way could resort, if grudgingly, to their cars as an alternative, the cottagers and campers of the Deer Lake area could not. The train was their only access; these land owners, most of them elderly, were in effect forced to abandon their cabins, which because inaccessible had become nearly worthless.

Recreation stations are not yet a thing of the past. The world's longest passenger train attests to that. Every morning during the summer, the renowned and popular Agwa Canyon tour train drags as many as eighteen passenger coaches away from the Algoma Central Railway Station in Sault Ste Marie, on a day-long train ride to the spectacular mountain passes and gorges of Algoma. Deep in the Agawa Canyon it deposits the awe-struck tourists onto the platform of Canyon Station, a converted section house. Here they hike to waterfalls, picnic by the river, take pictures of the soaring canyon walls, or just inhale the clean air and the silence of this remote region.

A smaller gaggle of nature lovers climb aboard the ACR's local train at the Frater Station for a shorter ride to the same location. The local train, which covers the entire ACR line between Sault Ste Marie and Hearst, also carries cottagers and fishermen to the remote lakes that line the route where they disembark at tiny wooden "umbrella" stations to bask in true remoteness, where the only way out is the train that is disappearing down the tracks.

The Ontario Northland Railway also promotes its "Polar Bear Express" from Cochrane to Moosonee. The opportunity to see this Cree community and Moose Factory, Ontario's oldest "European" settlement, attracts more than 40,000 travellers each summer. In response to the growing demand, the town of Cochrane has converted the upstairs of the CN/ONR station into a motel. Downstairs, the traditional station functions such as baggage check-in, ticketing, and even a lunch counter are part of one of a very few such traditional stations left in the country.

Ski Trains

Not all Canadian recreation is summer sport. During the 1920s in the steep, spectacular Laurentian Mountains north of Montreal, the sport of skiing suddenly surged to the fore.

It was through these same mountains that the Montreal, Ottawa and Western Railway (renamed the Montreal and Western) had in 1891 opened a colonization line as far as Ste Adele, and in 1909 to Mont Laurier. The original purpose of the line was to help the government of Quebec and the Roman Catholic church implement their joint policy of colonizing the relatively fertile mountain valleys with settlers from the overcrowded parishes of the St. Lawrence valley.

A string of stations, many copying the earlier QM and O style, were constructed at villages like Shawbridge, Val David, and St. Faustin. While the long and snowy winters made pioneering life difficult for the early settlers, they had considerable appeal to a ski enthusiast named Herman Johannsen. Born in Horten, Norway, in 1875, Johannsen immigrated to Canada in 1919 and became a salesman of engineering equipment. But the best skier of his time in Norway soon devoted his time to that sport in his adopted country as well. In 1920, better known as "Jack Rabbit" Johannsen, he cut the Maple Leaf trail between Shawbridge and Mont Tremblant, a distance of sixty miles, and turned the Laurentians into a skier's mecca.

In 1975 a special "Jack Rabbit" ski train, laid on to celebrate Johannsen's one hundredth birthday, carried more than a thousand skiers to Val David. Sensing the resurging popularity of the train as a way to avoid crowded and treacherous highways, the

One of Canada more famous railway experiences is the train ride to the magnificent Agawa Canyon in northern Ontario. Here passengers board the local train at Canyon station.

Skiers tumble from the CPR ski train at St Marguerite Station in the Laurentians. Beginning during the 1930s, the trains to Mont Laurier began to bulge with skiers, and for many years thereafter the "Petit Train du Nord" was a popular Quebec institution. Although the train departed Montreal daily, the Friday ski train was what everyone waited for. Up to twelve cars would leave Montreal's Park Avenue Station behind the puffing steam locomotives, dropping skiers at stations such as Mt. Tremblant and St. Agathe. By 1960, however, the province of Quebec had carried its highway construction programs deep into the Laurentians, and trains dropped to three a week.

Laurentian Regional Development Council and the local tourist association restored the train service, and once more skiers tumbled out at their favourite station.

Then on November 15, 1981, Transport Minister Jean Luc Pepin, insensitive to the needs and wishes of Montreal skiers, eliminated the train. Johannsen outlived the ski train and skied until he died at the age of 114 in 1989. In 1988 the CPR finally ended all train service into the area and abandoned the line.

Montreal was not the only city where skiers enjoyed the proximity to Quebec's mountains. Another pioneering line of the Montreal and Western snaked from Ottawa through the Gatineaus of Quebec to the lumber town of Maniwaki. In between lay a landscape of snow-covered mountains and hills. Here too skiers crowded onto trains that took them to such renowned ski resort towns as Wakefield. While passenger service had ended by the early 1960s, summer steam excursions continued to Wakefield, the line's sole surviving station.

Ontario's hills offered another skiers' paradise. Although the hills were neither as inviting nor as close to the large cities as those of the Laurentians in Quebec, Ontario nonetheless boasted its own ski trains. Overlooking the blue waters of Georgian Bay ten kilometres west of Collingwood are the Blue Mountains. By the 1930s ski trails had been carved into the forested faces of the slopes. On weekends ski trains from Toronto would chug through Collingwood and puff to a halt in front of the tiny, turreted Craigleith station, where the skiers were whisked away by horse-drawn sleighs to the primitive ski lodges. The ski trains ended in 1966, and the tracks were lifted shortly thereafter. The Craigleith station survives as a popular local restaurant, especially for skiers, who now must travel by car and can only envy their predecessors' relaxed travel in the ski trains.

During the late 1960s a commercial jingle floated from the radio urging skiers to take the "first train to Huntsville," another poplar ski region. But this rephrasing of the hit record "Take the Last Train to Clarkesville" fell victim to the car craze and corporate hostility to passenger trains, and soon disappeared from the airwaves as surely as the ski trains disappeared from the rails.

Red Lights

Although the fact is seldom mentioned in local histories, the most popular form of recreation associated with Canada's larger stations was prostitution. While most eastern cities already had red-light districts before the arrival of the railways, the brothels of western Canada came with the railway and were located close to the station.

In most western railway towns the main street ended at the back door of the station. The hookers, however, preferred to stay out of sight. To avoid citizen protest and police scrutiny they tended to locate on side streets that led off the main drag.

Few of the smaller towns were bothered by prostitution. As one prairie pioneer recalls, "Our town was pretty small; it only had one brothel." The occasional overnighting salesman or travelling preacher was seldom enough to warrant a full-blown red-light district.

Instead the hookers headed for the divisional towns. Here they were sure to find restless train crews looking for ways to fill the hours until their return shift, passengers waiting for the train to be serviced, or travelling salesmen yearning for companionship while waiting for a connecting train.

One of western Canada's most boisterous brothel towns was Saskatoon. When, only a few years apart, the Canadian Northern, the Canadian Pacific, and the Grand Trunk Pacific all laid rails into what had until then been a tiny prairie outpost, the place became a boom town. Young single men flocked into the growing settlement confident of finding work; salesmen funnelled in and out on the many lines that radiated from the town.

It was a hooker's haven. Between the CNR station and the river, 20th and 21st streets became a twenty-four-hour parade of men, "painted women" often hurling abuse behind them.

Compared to this wild west, prostitution played a relatively minor role around eastern Canada's stations. Older and better established, eastern Canada's were family towns, without large populations of young and restless men. But the hookers were there, although they rarely frequented the stations themselves. Young men with oats to sow had only to ask a cab driver for directions to the nearest brothel.

Pimps, however, were a problem in the large urban stations. Here they would lurk in the concourses—Toronto's Union Station was a favourite—and carefully scan the arriving crowds for unaccompanied young girls, naive and vulnerable, many of whom were fleeing the crushing boredom and predictability of life in rural Canada to seek money and independence in the big cities. Once in the hands of the pimps, however, they became little more than slaves. The Travellers Aid Society, working with railway security and plainclothes police, were in the stations too, ready to pounce upon pimps before they could claim their prey.

Far from the cities in the remote railway towns and the mining camps of northern Ontario and Quebec, the proportionately high male population brought with it the expected gaggle of painted ladies.

Biscotasing, north of Sudbury, Ontario, during its early years was a divisional point and construction camp for the CPR. Here the hookers' two-room shacks, known as "cribs," crowded the dirt lanes close to the station. The pimping, the drinking, and the gambling turned the little shanty town into a wild-and-woolly frontier outpost. Within a few years, however, the construction crews had moved on, and the CPR moved its divisional point to Chapleau. Again the red lights followed, and Biscotasing settled down to become a more sedate and sober mill town.

Sudbury, Ontario, was originally called Sudbury Junction the point at which the two branches of the CPR met the short-lived Algoma Eastern Railway. Here the CPR built large yards, repair shops, and a large divisional headquarters. Behind the CPR station along Elgin Street a string of hotels appeared where train crews and travellers alike could find accommodating companionship.

Sudbury remains a busy divisional point. Although the prostitution trade has largely disappeared, many of the hotels still stand and suffer yet from a lingering reputation of having once been the less savory part of town.

Railway towns from coast to coast were the same, although history seldom reflects this colourful era. Most are quiet now. As the towns grew, more families moved in. The young men married and settled down to raise families. The end of prohibition diverted the hookers from the brothels into the taverns. Then the depression, with its lower salaries and hoards of unemployed, meant few had money to spare. By the start of the Second World War the station red-light districts had nearly vanished from the landscape. Prostitution will continue to flourish, albeit in less obvious ways. However, its days when the hookers were just a few paces from the back doors of the stations have ended forever.

Moose Jaw was one of the towns where illicit pleasure flourished. Although the CPR first built its maintenance shops in Regina, where a red-light district immediately popped up around the corner of 10th and Ottawa streets, the railway relocated its divisional facilities to Moose Jaw, and most of the hookers followed. The red-light district there was concentrated along River Street west of the main street and just a block north of the busy station. Here, in a string of hotels, bars, and restaurants, the flesh trade was plied. Moose Jaw became Regina's red-light district as well, and during American prohibition gained a reputation as a hide-out for American rum runners. As this photo shows, many of the hotels from that era survive; they now enjoy a rather more sedate existence.

The Railway Ys

The inclination of railway crews to tumble off the trains at the end of their run and toddle off to the taverns or the "tarts" was viewed with considerable concern by the railway companies. Not only was the practice giving the railways a poor reputation, but the crews were showing up for their return shifts in less than desirable shape. As a result, the railways along with the Young Men's Christian Association started a series of railway YMCAs, located at divisional points, to give the crews a home away from home and keep them out of the bars and brothels. In many of Canada's larger railway towns the railway YMCA was a sight and activity as much a part of the station as the garden, the waiting room, or the water tank.

Founded in London, England, in 1844 to provide youthful workers with an alternative to the depressing and dirty urban environment created by the Industrial Revolution, the YMCA first appeared in North America in Montreal in 1851. The first informal links to the railways began in 1866 at Point St. Charles near Montreal, where the huge Grand Trunk yards employed twelve hundred men. The first formal association for railway workers was formed at St. Thomas, Ontario, in 1881.

But it was out along the remote sections of the main line that the crews faced horrible conditions. Accommodation often consisted of cold and barren bunkhouses, some of them converted boxcars. In 1896 D. A. Budge, general secretary of the Montreal YMCA, visited the Grand Trunk Railway's divisional points, in 1906 those of the CPR. The dreadful conditions that he witnessed on these tours so disturbed him that he resolved to provide workers with comfortable beds and a Christian environment, and to do this by establishing a string of hostels run by the YMCA. Money was scarce and existing structures had to be converted for the first Ys.

The first structure of any size to become a railway Y was the former Canada Northern office at the foot of Toronto's Spadina Avenue. The Grand Trunk fitted the building with a dormitory, a small gym, a restaurant, baths, and an outside play area, and turned it over to the Y.

The program soon became a huge success. Within twenty years twenty-eight railway Ys were in place. Built and owned by the railways, they were staffed by the Y and offered theatre, cards, bowling, and bible reading. They were comfortable and warm and welcomed by the lonely crew members. All were located at the larger railway yards, such as Revelstoke, Cranbrook, and Field in B.C., Moose Jaw in Saskatchewan, and Moncton in New Brunswick. In Ontario railway Ys were scattered through the north at Sioux Lookout, Capreol, Cartier, Chapleau, Hornepayne, Ignace, Kenora, Schreiber, and White River and in the south at Allandale (Barrie), Fort Erie, Niagara Falls, St. Thomas, Sarnia, and Stratford. Four were located in Toronto and three in Montreal. There was even a Canadian railway Y in the U.S., located at the CPR's Brownville Junction in Maine.

Many of the railway communities were small and remote and enjoyed few social or recreational facilities. Here the railway Ys quickly became the centre for dances, teas, bake sales, and movies.

As with much of Canada's railway traditions and scenes, the end began in 1960 with dieselization. Because the diesel engines no longer had to stop every two hundred and fifty miles to change the water in the boilers, the crews bypassed many of the old divisional points. Where layovers did continue, the railways built their own bunkhouses with larger rooms and more modern facilities.

In the larger towns the Ys were turned over to the community. In smaller places this was not feasible, and the railways, still the owners of the buildings, demolished them. The Ignace Y was demolished in 1967. That in Sioux Lookout, one of the largest, became railway offices, with new bunkhouses added. Then in 1989 the CNR pulled most of its crew out of Sioux Lookout and demolished the building, which had been one of the largest and most substantial in this northwestern Ontario outpost. A few former railway Ys still stand and enjoy other uses. That at Allandale, a fine nineteenth-century brick building, is now a hotel and popular lounge. Only that at White River, altered following a fire, still accommodates train crews.

Crews still lay over, and they are still lonely, but today they relax in modern motel-like bunkhouses. Most have forgotten, and perhaps many never knew, of the days when the railway Y stood just behind the station and was their home away from home.

***

And so, whether it was to enjoy a fine meal, unload a canoe or skis, sleep over, or pursue less savory activities, Canada's stations were often a gateway to recreation; recreation that, for the most part, the railway companies promoted and capitalized on, even to the point of creating special station designs. But, with only a few exceptions, it is just another of those many once-loved station functions that survives only in the memories of those that lived it.

Many of the railway Ys were large and architecturally attractive. That at Sioux Lookout (shown here) was three storeys high, constructed of brick in the beaux arts style, and contained a two-lane bowling alley, a fireplace, lecture rooms, and library. The stone Y at Ignace had tennis courts, a verandah, a reading room, and a horseshoe pitch. In Field, B.C., the Mount Stephen House hotel was converted into a Y and replaced in 1935 by a larger structure that contained the station as well. The Sioux Lookout building was demolished in 1989.

Middleton, Nova Scotia

Amqui, Quebec

Prevost, Quebec

Mount Rolland, Quebec

Pictou, Nova Scotia

Kensington, Prince Edward Island

St. Bruno, Quebec

Kentville, Nova Scotia

Avondale, Newfoundland

what do you think of Little York aug 2 - 1906 a picture of the crowd went to play football how do you like. Auntie Maggie another little girl at alfreds Ida is all right Good bye. George

Metropolitan Toronto Reference Library T-12196

The Station was Their Stage: The Railway Station in Small-Town Canada

To three generations of small-town Canadians the station was the heart of the community. Here they met, worshipped, socialized, danced, and even married. They gathered to greet teary-eyed relatives or to bid fearful farewells to soldier sons. They cheered royalty and jeered politicians. They congregated on the station platform to meet the mail, crowded into the waiting room to hear the news on the telegraph, or strolled by just to see who was arriving. The station was their stage.

Many of the station memories that Canadians cherish the most were those obtained as children. To a child the lure of the station was irresistible.

I grew up in North Toronto, an area with an urban population that preferred to move

in cars or TTC buses. The closest station to us was the CPR station in Leaside. Although few passenger trains used it—and we certainly never did—our most eagerly anticipated summer entertainment was to drive to that station and watch the shining black steam engines puff and hiss past, dragging a load of creaking, lurching freight cars. Of course, this was before we bought a TV. But there was just something about a station.

In an early version of today's "hanging out at the mall," youngsters all across Canada would buy their candies at the local store and then bicycle, skip, or run to the station to meet their friends. Then when the daily train arrived, all attention was on the hissing coaches. Curious eyes would peer cautiously into the baggage car to see if any convicts lurked in its dark recesses, chained glumly to the wall. In late summer they would skulk around the station to catch the first glimpse of a newly arriving teacher.

If a train from the United States was to pass, as often happened in southern Ontario and Quebec, an ambitious youth might persuade a vendor to part with a prized American newspaper. For those brief moments he was the centre of attention, for in his hands was the news of those faraway and forbidden cities south of the border. Others would push and shove towards the travelling salesmen, outshouting each other with offers to carry his heavy satchel to the hotel, usually just across the dusty street, for a nickel or a dime.

In a Canada that knew nothing of TVs or public playgrounds, the station became the entertainment for town youngsters, usually to the annoyance of the agent. When games of chase around the platform wore out, or when the agent shooed them off, the gang might scramble to the water tank and climb to its lofty summit, or turn the hand-operated turntable into a slow-motion and creaking merry-go-round. Many youngsters would experience

their first train ride by boarding secretly at the coal dock or water tank and riding the train to the station, just a few yards away. In quieter and more curious moods they would simply watch the agent carry out his daily duties, peeking from beneath a desk to watch him clack out a message on his telegraph key, or peering around the corner of the station as he manipulated the baggage carts over the wooden platform.

Sometimes the station was their escape, their gateway to the world outside. Youngsters would hurry to the station, often hours early, coins clutched in their hands, and fidget impatiently until a distant whistle announced the train that would carry them to town to see the current movie, or to the crowd and commotion of the local fair.

When the sultry summer nights gave way to the cool winds of fall, the station lost much of its allure. For those of high-school age fall meant bundling up against the morn-

(far left) Though abandoned, the Wawa Ontario station is an irresistible lure for young Jeri and Ria.

(left) Craigleith. Stations were where loved ones reunited, especially at Christmas.

ing chill, to trudge to the darkened depot and await the distant light of the train that would take them to school.

As youth bloomed into adulthood courtship blossomed at many a country station. Young couples would walk, hand in hand if they dared, down the main street and past darkened shops to the station, where a setting sun would turn the rails into golden ribbons. As the sun inched below the horizon they might walk along the rails, balancing awkwardly, until one would slip onto the cinders and both would laugh.

Some evenings other couples would join them. If someone had brought a harmonica and if the agent had children of like age, then all might crowd into the waiting room. Simple tunes would fill the air and boots would clomp a two-step upon the shiny oiled floors. From such evenings love often bloomed, and many a marriage took place within a railway station.

Every generation had its youthful troublemakers. A frustrated newspaper reporter despaired of the antics around the Central Ontario Railway station at Gilmour, Ontario: it was "as is no other place in the north...well stocked with uncontrolled drunkenness...a Saturday, even Sunday, drunks pitching quoits and shooting at a target...attempts at train wrecking have been made several times at the station."

The greatest lure, however, was the mail. After the mail-car clerk handed the bags to the agent and the agent to the postmaster, a throng of people would follow the latter to the station or post office, anxious to clutch the long-awaited, perhaps perfumed, love letter, the newspaper from the old country, or the latest Eaton's catalogue. At Christmas the carts bulged with parcels that contained gifts of fruits, cakes, and toys.

The station's role could extend beyond the secular. Although stores and hotels were quick to follow the railways into virgin territory, churches took longer. A congregation had to organize, had to let the church headquarters know of their existence, and had somehow to find the money to build their first church buildings. Until then, many a railway station served as the community's first "church." Reverend Silas Huntington, whose territory in the 1880s and 1890s included the CPR lands in northern Ontario, was frequently forced to preach in railway stations, lamenting that "such places are not suitable for our evangelistic work."

One of the northern Ontario stations used for church services was the one at Franz, where the main line of the CPR crossed the busy Algoma Central. The lower half of the ticket agent's door served as an altar from which the travelling Anglican priest had ardent parishioners and hapless passengers alike.

Ken Liddell recalls that in Peebles, Saskatchewan, worshippers at first found nowhere to worship and resorted to the station water tank. Sheltered from the elements by a wooden exterior wall, and heated by a stove that was intended to keep the water from freezing, they huddled against the curving wall to sing their praises to the Lord, and perhaps offered a silent prayer that no hissing steam engine would rumble alongside and lower the creaking and leaky spout to fill its boilers and douse the worshippers.

Meanwhile, in Quebec, where the railway had come long after the village cathedrals had pointed their silver steeples skyward, the village curé, black robed and fingering his beads, could be seen pacing the station platform to greet arriving villagers and visitors alike.

Before the prairies filled with pioneers who shunted Canada's Indians onto reserves, the stations became a lure for native people. At first simply curious at the puffing and belching steam engines, they quickly began to recognize the commercial potential of train time and of their own attraction to tourists. In his 1887 account of a cross-country train trip, W.H. Withrow recalled how "at many of the stations a few Indians or half breeds may be seen.... They were selling buffalo horns from which rough and outer surface had been chipped or filed off."

Then came trainloads of immigrants to push aside the natives. It was from the station platforms that 3 million Canadians first saw their new homelands. There were Americans who found their own frontiers closed

(above) The original Winnipeg station was a major gathering spot for immigrants heading west.

(above right) Considered by some to pose a security threat during the early years of World War 2, these Japanese-Canadians are on their way to internment camps in British Columbia's remote ghost towns.

(above far right) The CPR's first transcontinental train brought out the military to the Qu'Appelle, Saskatchewan station in 1886.

after 1900, the English and Scots who were shut out of their own industrial revolution, and Clifford Sifton's "stalwart peasants in sheepskin coats" from Eastern Europe.

For more than ten years, from 1886 to 1896, the CPR held 25 million acres of prime prairie wheatland. A world-wide recession, however, slowed sales and the railway began rigorously pursuing foreign immigration. Clifford Sifton, the federal minister responsible for immigration between 1896 and 1904, joined the CPR in touting the fertility of the West. It worked. Between 1896 and 1914 more than 3 million immigrants piled into the immigration sheds at Quebec, Saint John, or Halifax, or they trekked from Montana to the western Canadian wheatlands.

In April 1893 the *Quebec Chronicle* described 400 immigrants tumbling off the ship *SS Lake Huron* and into the Levis station across the river from Quebec City. The 1000 pieces of luggage that they had were placed on disinfection cars and wheeled into the disinfection room. Here the doors were sealed and boilers heated water to 230 degrees to steam the contents.

While waiting, the immigrants could visit the special ticket office and exchange onward steamer tickets for railway tickets. A large dining hall on the wharf sold, in addition to meals, food items that the immigrants might need for their long train ride to the awaiting west.

The railways were the immigrants' way to the prairies and the stations played key roles all along the route. The trains plucked them from immigration sheds and carried them in crowded colonist cars to the Winnipeg CPR station. Here the immigrants huddled about their belongings, waiting for an immigration official who spoke their language to direct them to the immigration hall. There they would find food, beds, and tools to get them started at their new homesteads. But also stalking the station were unscrupulous boarding house operators who, under the comforting cloak of being fellow countrymen, whisked the new arrivals away to overpriced boarding houses; never bothering to tell them that similar accommodation was available in the government immigration halls—free.

Then there was the final station destination. Many immigrants had purchased their farms before leaving home, others at the land offices in the west. But that first look at their "home station" was always the most

difficult. At some, the agent took them in and gave them room and board and helped them locate their homestead. At others there was no agent and sometimes only a boxcar or a shed for a station. Here they would disembark and, in bewilderment, look around at the bald and unsettled grassland—no town, not even another farm in sight—and wonder where their path led—or even where their path lay.

After a time most adapted to their new conditions and settled into farming or running small businesses. They, as others before them, began to look to their stations for a variety of things. One of them was the telegraph.

Prior to the radio and the telephone, the station telegraph brought the residents of many Canadian communities their daily news. When the telegraph was not clacking

with train orders, it might be sending out the latest grain prices, vital to the prairie communities, or the latest weather. During elections the men of the community crowded into the smoky waiting room to cheer the latest victory or defeat of John A. MacDonald or Wilfred Laurier.

Sports events such as the Stanley Cup playoffs, the World Series, or a heavyweight fight drew even larger crowds into the station.

The war years brought news that shook many communities. Following the bloody fighting at Dieppe and Ypres, the telegraph clicked out the names of sons or husbands killed on the sodden battlefields of France and Belgium. In Canada's small towns the grief of one family was shared by all. One station, near Base Borden, Ontario, was renamed Ypres, following the horrific battle near that village.

Isolation drew people even closer to their station. In the pre-highway era road travel between most communities was rugged and slow; but travel between the tiny station villages in northern Ontario and Quebec did not exist. Dense swamps, swirling rivers, and the world's hardest rock turned back any attempt at settlement apart from the railway towns. Here the station was the residents' lifeline, their only contact with the outside. So isolated and small were these tiny train towns that most lacked dentists, doctors, or schools, services taken for granted in the towns and villages of the south.

One man saw the inequity and cared. In 1922 J.B. McDougall, a North Bay school inspector, convinced the Ontario Department of Education to experiment with a rolling school house. Between 1926 and 1967 the government joined hands with the CNR, the CPR, and the Temiskaming and Northern Ontario Railway (later the Ontario Northland Railway) to convert seven passenger coaches into classrooms.

These classrooms-on-wheels were equipped with desks, books, blackboards, and living quarters for the teacher and his family. They were hauled on the back of a train, unceremoniously at times, back and forth along a predetermined stretch of railway line where they were backed onto sidings to spend a week at the smallest communities. From the camps and cabins of the Cree and Ojibway, from the shacks of the trappers, and from the trackside houses of the railway section gangs the children would emerge, books and homework in hand, often tramping along miles of dense forest trails, ready for another week of lessons.

But the teacher's job did not end with the afternoon bell. Most evenings adults from the community would crowd the coach to learn arithmetic, English, or just pick up the latest news of an outside world that they so seldom saw. Many teachers devoted their lives to their tasks: the late Fred Sloman of Clinton, Ontario, for example, was Canada's longest-serving school-car teacher, teaching from his school car north of Capreol, Ontario, for nearly the entire duration of the program.

Struck by the success of the rolling school cars, the Ontario Department of Health created rolling dentists' offices. Although they spent less time in each community, the two dental cars rattled back and forth along fifteen hundred miles of CN trackage and thirteen hundred miles of the CPR.

By the late 1960s highways had reached Ontario's remotest railway villages, and the school cars and dental cars were backed onto

Provincial Archives of Alberta B6102

sidings and forgotten. One school car has been preserved at the Canadian Railway Museum at Delston, Quebec; Fred Sloman's school car, spotted by chance sitting derelict on a storage siding, was rescued from the scrap yard to become a museum in Sloman's hometown of Clinton, Ontario.

In the days before television and all-night cinemas the station was where the townspeople went to be entertained. Whether they went to gasp at royalty, to jeer at politicians, or to hail conquering sports heros, the station was where it happened.

The first such event for any station was the opening of the station itself and the arrival of its first train. Bands, banners, and politicians were all on hand to herald a new era for their community.

These often turned into community fêtes and were lavishly covered by the local press. The opening of the Great Western station in Hamilton on January 23, 1854 saw, according to the *Toronto Globe*, "Every stage, steamboat, and Railroad train...loaded with guests; the hotels were crowded to excess and the merry groups on the streets showed that the entire population was in a high state of excitement with approaching celebration."

Festivities marking the opening of the London and Port Stanley Railway in 1856 lasted four days. According to the *London Herald* of October 17, 1856, "In the morning [London] presented an animated appearance, flags flying and firemen in their various uniforms parading the streets. About 10 o'clock they formed into a procession and proceeded to

Glenbow Archives ND-3-5991

(left) Station openings often drew crowds; here Edmonton's CN station is officially opened, 1928.

(right) Unknown today, J.J. Maloney, the head of the Canadian Ku Klux Klan, drew the curious to Alberta's stations during the early 1930s; he ended up in jail.

the Port Stanley Railway Station on Bathurst Street, where the station house and the cars were tastefully decorated with green arches."

A correspondent accompanying the first transcontinental train of the CPR in June 1886 recalls that it was an occasion that brought the townspeople flocking to the station. At Winnipeg the militia fired a salvo of artillery as the train rolled into the station. The mayor gave a welcoming speech, and crowds piled through the coaches.

Further west at Swift Current, the correspondent noted that the arrival of the first train had attracted a number of local Indians to the station: "Mr. Red Skin showed up in all his glory of blankets of various colours, trappings and leathers...one Indian boy had his pony on the platform and rode it about for inspection."

At the Crowfoot station a celebrity was waiting for the train. "The great chief of the Blackfeet, Crowfoot, came to meet us at the station named after himself. He is a good-looking old Indian, sharp featured, black hair and bright eyes. We composed an address to him interpreted by a clergyman we found at the station...the old fellow expressed his 'ughs' of satisfaction."

Canada's first troop trains were drawing cheering well-wishers and tearful family members to the station even before the CPR had finished its continental link. In 1885 Montrealers jammed the hillside that overlooked Dalhousie Square Station to wave at and cheer the troops being sent to crush Louis Riel's second rebellion. The horrendous difficulties in sending troops to counter Riel's first uprising a decade earlier, when there

was no railway, had awakened the government to the need for quick completion of the CPR syndicate's on-again, off-again transcontinental railway. Cheering Winnipegers greeted the militia as they clustered on the platform of the Winnipeg station, while still another throng met them at the Qu'Appelle station as they made ready to march out after the rebels.

At the battle of Ridgeway during the 1870 Fenian raids into southern Ontario, a pair of stations played a military role. To counter the Americans who had landed at Fort Erie and were advancing westward, the Canadians massed eight hundred troops at Port Colborne Station and boarded flatcars to Ridgway, where they engaged the Fenians. During the battle the Americans gained the upper hand and forced the Canadians back to

the Ridgeway station, where they hurried back onto the train and retreated to Port Colborne.

Some of the most moving moments at any railway station were the tearful farewells to troops during the two world wars. Troops massed at the stations closest to the military bases to board the trains that would eventually take them to the Atlantic ports, and then perhaps onward to a muddy grave in the trenches of France or Belgium, or to die on a bouldery beach at Normandy. Stations like Orillia and Whitby, Toronto's Exhibition Station, or Camp Borden, which had two stations of its own, were the focus for troop farewells.

As the wars progressed the stations hosted arrivals of a different kind. In Europe, as the

German war machine began to crumble, prisoners were marched onto ships and back to POW camps in Canada. Many of them were processed in Quebec, where they were transferred onto trains that would take them to northern Ontario communities such as Kapuskasing, the site of a large POW camp.

Not all wartime prisoners were the enemy. Fostered by flimsy fears that were fanned by racism, the federal government on February 24, 1941, passed its infamous order in council PC 1486 that ordered the RCMP to round up Canadians of Japanese origin, confiscate their property, and inter them. After first being processed at Hastings Park in Vancouver, they were hustled onto eastbound trains. Many were hurried off the trains and onto the platform of the New Denver, B.C., station,

from where they were allocated to the ghost towns of Kaslo, Slocan, Greenwood, or Sandon. Others were kept on the train until it reached the Taber, Alberta, station, where ruddy-faced sugar-beet farmers met them and escorted them to the farms where they would toil long hours in the fields. Still others ended up in Ontario at a remote ghost town, then stationless, on the CNR named Tionaga.

Finally, the war over, the stations thronged with happier crowds, wives holding high their children for the first glimpse of the father they had never seen, and mothers who had sent a boy to war and welcomed home a hardened hero.

The end of World War II also brought with it a new breed of immigrant—the war bride. Thousands married—or became engaged to—Canadian soldiers stationed in England. When the war ended they thronged onto steamships bound for Canada. Here they were taken by train to their respective destinations, escorted by army officials and released only when their spouses signed their custodial care papers. Station scenes were often chaotic—anxious brides disappearing into crowds before the papers were completed. On occasion they were tragic; the bride standing forlornly with no one there to meet her.

Another western farming institution, now forgotten, was the annual trek of eastern farm labourers to the western crop harvest. In the late 1890s western settlers were reaping their first crop and discovering that vital farm labour was nowhere to be found. Meanwhile, back east, the harvest was finished and farm labourers had time on their hands.

To help the western harvest, and, not incidentally, help in their promotion of prairie

(above left) Canadian troops depart for the front during World War II in high spirits.

(above) Edmontonians envelop the CP station to welcome home World War I veterans of the 49th Battalion.

lands, the CPR began advertising for farm help. The harvest trains, known as harvester specials, were an instant success. Despite the long train ride in old colonist coaches and the 16-hour days, the harvesters found the fares low ($12) and the wages high (up to $18 per day).

At the eastern stations platforms were piled high with the harvesters' luggage, while at western stations the farmers surged forward, each one anxious to hire strong hands lest his crops remain standing.

Following the first war, the federal Department of Labour took over recruitment—by this time the government railways were moving harvesters too. By 1920 the railways carried nearly half a million harvesters. But, after 1929, drought and depression combined

to put an end to the harvester specials.

In times of peace and prosperity, Canadians flocked to the station for the arrival of special trains. Some were educational. In 1901 A.W. "Good Roads" Campbell coordinated a "Good Roads" train full of the latest road-making equipment, destined for a variety of southern Ontario towns and village. His efforts to encourage better roads by using the train was an irony that none would understand until decades later, when roads brought about the downfall of rail service. In 1913 a "Made in Canada" train toured the stations of the CPR. Canadians flocked to the stations to see the variety of products then made in Canada. (Free trade deals might today prohibit a repeat of such a train.) And every June and July between 1915 and 1918 the Saskatchewan College of Agriculture sent out the "Better Farming" train to the many stations throughout rural Saskatchewan. The train carried exhibits of livestock, field crops, and farm machinery.

In 1936 the CPR celebrated the fiftieth anniversary of its first transcontinental train by sending its special jubilee train out west. More than two thousand people turned up at Regina's imposing union station to greet the train there. As it rolled into the Moose Jaw station, engines in the massive yard let out a cacophony of hoots and whistles, completely drowning out the efforts of the Canadian Legion band to entertain the travelling dignitaries milling about the station platform. Among the thousand who lined the platform at Portage la Prairie stood one Fred Newman, who had been at Craigellachie for the driving of the last spike more than fifty years before.

Saskatchewan Archives R-B 3751-3

In 1948 the Edmonton Chamber of Commerce sponsored a special friendship train to visit the remote communities of the Peace River country. With eighty Edmonton businessmen on board, the train passed through several little agricultural towns. The greeting at Slave Lake Station was typical. Here the travellers were met by a huge throng that launched into a spontaneous sing-song and dance on the station's rickety wooden platform.

In 1953 the CNR's special museum train drew thousands of Canadians to the stations to see the vintage coaches and wood-burning locomotives. Fourteen years later the federal government's confederation train crossed the country with its displays and decorations.

Some of the largest and most ecstatic crowds to beseige the stations were those who welcomed home their sports heros. Early

in Canada's history, as towns battled each other for supremacy on the soccer field or the skating pond, it was the trains that carried the teams home to the station where crowds waited to cheer them. Screaming fans would choke Montreal's Windsor Station or Toronto's Union Station to roar their adulation as the Leafs or Canadiens brought home the coveted Stanley Cup.

For many years Toronto remained the site of the Grey Cup, and each year trains from the West would disgorge into the Union Station concourse cheering, hollering, occasionally staggering football fans, a tradition that would continue until other cities built large stadiums and until airplanes took over from the trains.

The high point of the Grey Cup train rides, however, was the 1955 Grey Cup "Goodwill" train. Led by Metropolitan

Toronto's first chairman, Fred Gardiner, two hundred politicians, businessmen, cheerleaders, and just plain football fans paraded down Yonge Street to Union Station and onto the special train that would carry them across the country to the site of the Grey Cup; this time in Vancouver.

At the Winnipeg station the goodwill ambassadors were met by mayor George Sharpe. There they formed up in the waiting room to parade down Main Street. Outside the warm station they battled winds of thirty-five miles per hour that whipped up the foot of fresh snow and made the bone-chilling temperatures of twelve degrees fahrenheit feel more like twenty below. The hardy revellers met similar conditions at Regina's station three days later, but gritted their teeth and launched yet another parade. Their spirits were so high that newspaper writer Val Sears

(left) Nicknamed the "Weed Train", the Saskatchewan Government's rolling classroom offered crop displays and farming seminars.

(right) Football fans wish their Stampeders well in their quest for the 1948 Grey Cup. In that year fans of the Canadian Football League's Calgary team added a new dimension to station celebrations. Their beloved Stamps were to battle the Ottawa Roughriders at Toronto's Varsity Stadium, and to urge the players on, the fans brought a little bit of the West with them. Toronto residents gaped as the Calgarians unloaded their horses and their chuckwagons and turned Union Station into a scene of pancake breakfasts, square dancing, country sing-alongs, and good old-fashioned Grey Cup whoop-ups. The "Stampeder Special" became and instant institution. In 1949, with the Stampeders once again in the Grey Cup, Calgarians jammed 15 coaches. The cP added an extra baggage car where the fiddles and guitars filled the air with square dance music. All along the route, wherever a long stop was scheduled, crowds gathered at the station to cheer on the team—who were in the train ahead—and then to clap their hands to the music of the revellers.

enthused, "Not since World War Two has there been a train like this one. It may possibly make railway history."

One of Canada's longest-standing traditions and one of its biggest station attractions has been the royal tour. Ever since Albert Edward, Prince of Wales, travelled past dozens of garlanded stations between Toronto and Collingwood in the 1860s, Canadians have jammed the stations to get a fleeting glimpse of royalty.

In 1901 when the Duke and Duchess of Cornwall and York took the CPR to Vancouver, reporters filled the pages with their glowing tributes to the royal couple. "It was a continual triumphant journey," gushed a CPR reporter, "the train dashing past gaily decorated stations. A brief stop was made at Three Rivers where an official welcome was extended the royal couple by the mayor. [In Montreal] a tremendous crowd of people occupied every available foot of space from which Place Viger Station could be seen."

A writer for the *Winnipeg Tribune* arrived early at that city's station. "Before the sun was up people began to assemble in the vicinity of the station...the 13th Field Battery thundered forth a royal salute." Thousands again jammed the station that evening when "rockets were sent high in the air as the train pulled out, and the scene was one long to be remembered."

In 1919 W.D. Newton, a British journalist, accompanied the Prince of Wales on his memorable cross-country tour of Canada. In his book *Westward with the Prince of Wales* he left vivid and stirring descriptions of the adulation at the stations. "At every station people were gathered. They had come sometimes from heaven knows where, for in the wide

No tour attracted more Canadians to their stations than did the Royal tour of 1939.

plain or the lonely valley there was no sign of habitation. They had come in by automobile or by rig or they had walked. They were content if all they could accomplish was to send a hearty cheer after the train as it sped by at express speed."

But the grandest royal tour of all was more leisurely and lured to the stations more Canadians than had ever assembled there before or since for a single event. This was the royal tour of 1939.

Never before had a reigning monarch visited Canada. Beginning in late May of 1939, King George VI and Queen Elizabeth (now Queen Mother Elizabeth) began their memorable cross-country train trip, a journey of more than three weeks. Special engines were

brought in and polished, and coaches were newly painted in royal blue and gold.

The tour began on May 17 in Quebec City and rolled westward along the CPR line. Fifty thousand cheering Quebeckers crowded the Trois Rivières station, sang "God Save the King," and cheered again when the Queen spoke to them in French. On May 22 the train made an unexpected stop at Brockville to greet the twenty-five thousand strong that engulfed the station.

As the train rolled on the crowds grew larger, undaunted by the time of night or the weather. "Never before has such a crowd gathered at one place in Belleville," noted the *Toronto Telegram*. "Early in the afternoon people started to take up positions along the barriers. By six o'clock fifteen thousand were at the station. Early in the evening rain started to fall but the crowd refused to leave."

Further west stands Cobourg. Here crowds began to gather at midnight, staying up all night; they were joined in the grey pre-dawn by the Cobourg Citizens' band. At 8:30 the train appeared, to a tumultuous roar, but rolled through without stopping, offering not even a glimpse of the royal couple.

At Toronto the royal couple disembarked at the CPR's former North Toronto Station to review a guard of honour. Officially closed a decade earlier, the grand station was re-opened for one day for the royal welcome.

When the King and Queen left Toronto thousands jammed the front of Union Station to send them off. But as the train rumbled through the farm country northwest of Toronto the station crowds were not so lucky. "At Kleinburg a group of five hundred watched in vain for a sight of their majesties," reported the *Telegram*. "The crowd included villagers, farmers, and cowboys in full western regalia from a nearby ranch. The only persons on the train who came into view were two coloured porters who waved towels at the crowd."

At stations like West Toronto, Weston, Woodbridge, Plagrave, Bolton, and even the now-vanished Blackhorse Crossing, the scene was repeated. Crowds jammed the tiny platforms, watching impatiently for the train that was an hour late, and then had to watch it roar through at sixty miles an hour.

As darkness fell that day the train squealed to a stop at Carley, north of Barrie, for water. Here a startling sight awaited the royal couple. Surrounding the station and parked on the hillside were a thousand automobiles, while higher on the hills were five piles of pine stumps ten feet high. As the King and Queen watched, the headlights came on and the pine piles were set ablaze. The King gazed in amazement at the spectacular show of lights; the Queen commented, "Aren't they beautiful? This is the prettiest sight of the trip."

Disappointment again greeted the crowds across Ontario's northland. A reporter with the pilot train noted, "As the train passes, lonely figures show by the track silently waiting for a flash of the royal special. At Franz Station a little crowd stood clustered waiting. They may be lucky to glimpse their two majesties if they do not sleep late."

White River, Ontario, residents were treated to a longer stopover. Natives canoed for days from their wilderness settlement to see the royal couple. "Shivering squaws with papooses bundled in their arms stood in snow to greet the King and Queen here today [May 23]," wrote the on-board reporter. "In Michipicoten near Puckasaw River a group of Indians one hundred miles away heard that the King and Queen might be in White River. They took to their canoes immediately over treacherous waters, all because the royal train is stopping here for twenty minutes." Trains from all around the northland—there were no roads—brought in people from outlying communities. It was the grandest twenty minutes the White River station would ever know.

The story was repeated all across the country, with thousands congregating at flag-bedecked stations in Regina, Calgary, and Vancouver. The train then made its way back along the CNR line through Jasper, Edmonton, Winnipeg again, and back into southern Ontario. Thousands converged upon the stations big and little. Many had come from far-away farms to spend an entire day in town, because for prairie kids a rare visit to Moose Jaw or Melville was almost as exhilarating as the sight of royalty was to their parents.

Two more royal visits brought Canadians out to the stations. In 1951 Princess Elizabeth and the Duke of Edinburgh spent a portion of their tour on the train, although much of it was by air. The queen-to-be retraced some of the ground covered by her parents twelve years earlier, pulling in crowds between Nova Scotia and Windsor, including thirty-five thousand at Cornwall and Brockville.

In 1978 some Canadians went to the station grounds (for by then many of the stations were gone) to witness royalty by rail for the last time. In token homage to the glorious tour by rail in 1939, Queen Elizabeth and Prince Phillip boarded a train in Regina and journeyed to four communities northeast of Regina. At the Fort Qu'Appelle station the Gordon Indian dancers entertained the royal party with a hoop dance and presented them with a ceramic plaque. Although the tour of '39 lasted three weeks, the Saskatchewan trip—the last time that Canadians would go to the station to see their Queen—was over in six and a half hours.

National Archives of Canada PA 136972

Pierre Trudeau revives the whistle-stop campaign, June, 1974.

(right) The Mulroney government's myopic obsession with rail passenger cutbacks in 1990 drew angry Canadians to their stations to demonstrate, as they did here at Medicine Hat.

If Canadians looked to their stations as the stage to cheer royalty, they equally saw it as an opportunity to give jeer to politicians.

In the days before radio and television, the only way a politician could really reach constituents was from the open end of a rail car. With only a few minutes to spend in each station, the candidate's organizers would hustle a crowd together, usually supporters, and assemble them at the stations. A few moments were spent listing accomplishments achieved and promises that would be kept, and the train would give a whistle and grunt and chug its way to the next station and the next cheering crowd of supporters.

Although it is likely that someone started "whistle-stopping" before John A. MacDonald came along, Canada's first prime minister is most closely identified with it. The CPR was after all his creation, and he used it to maximum advantage. There then followed Laurier, Bennett, and King, all reaching out to voters from vestibules.

Peter Newman, writing in the *Toronto Star*, suggests that John Diefenbaker was the last politician in history to campaign from the back of a train. As his 1965 campaign made its way through the farming communities of southern Saskatchewan, small crowds waited by the station to see the "Chief." At one stop, Mortlach, only four turned up, but a rousing welcome waited at the next stop, Morse. As over two hundred onlookers watched (most of them were high-school students who had been bussed in), Diefenbaker directed the local band through a march. Newman noted that "for some reason station agents in those days were musical (or thought they were) and organized ragged marching bands to welcome the Tory leader. Those of us in the train's press corps were constantly trying to file stories but seldom could, because the station agents were usually on the platform serenading the chief."

Funeral trains also drew Canadians to the station; to mourn and to pay last respects. The most memorable was that of Sir John A. MacDonald, who died on June 6, 1891 following a stroke. A reporter for the *Dominion Illustrated* magazine wrote this moving account of the funeral train as it passed various stations on its way to Kingston:

"As the train was leaving [Ottawa's CPR station] an old man, standing bareheaded on the platform, called out 'Good bye, Sir John, good bye'.... Stops were made at Carleton Place and Smiths Falls, where crowds of people pressed around the funeral car...at the lat-

Photo by Chuck Nisbett, courtesy of the Medicine Hat News

ter town a floral offering was made by the Liberal–Conservative association. At Perth no stop was made but the train passed through the station very slowly. The local band was in waiting and played the dead march as the cars went by.... The [Kingston] station...and the large square immediately opposite were densely crowded with citizens, eager to see the last home-coming of their illustrious representative." From the station, MacDonald's body was taken to Cataraqui for burial.

The funeral train of Sir John Diefenbaker was similar to that of MacDonald. In accordance with his wishes, Diefenbaker's remains were returned to Saskatchewan by train for burial. Like MacDonald's, the train drew huge crowds. Indeed, the crowd that mobbed the Kenora station was so huge that it forced the train to make an unscheduled stop.

The election of Pierre Trudeau ushered in the electronic age in politics. Although the famous Kennedy–Nixon TV debate had greatly influenced the outcome of the 1960 U.S. election, Canadians had to wait another eight years before Trudeaumania cast its spell through their TV screens.

Jet airlines replaced the trains, and the thirty-second "photo-op" replaced the five-minute whistle-stop. Nevertheless, Trudeau did engage in electioneering from the platform of a train. The 1974 election saw him make his way through a number of Maritime communities and dazzle the spectators from the platform of his coach.

But later crowds were not as friendly. In 1982 as Trudeau and his two sons made their way through western Canada on a vacation, an angry mob besieged the train at the station plat-

form in Salmon Arm, B.C. Trudeau responded by prominently showing the group his middle finger through the window of the train, later dubbed the "Salmon Arm Salute."

But the unfortunate PM's trial-by-mob didn't end there. When the residents of Canmore heard of Trudeau's gesture they mobbed the train throwing tomatoes and eggs. When the train eased into Sudbury station, the crowd was so hostile that the scheduled 40-minute stop was reduced to just a few minutes.

One of the most memorable station demonstrations of all occurred on the platform of Ontario's Brockville platform in 1989. September 6 was a hot and sticky day. Ontario premier David Peterson was due in town by train for a rally. Waiting for him amidst the Grit hacks and supporters were a number of "English-rights" groups there to oppose the premier's perceived support for bilingualism in Ontario.

After most of the demonstrators had dispersed and as the TV camera crews were packing up their equipment, a few remaining members of the groups laid the flag of Quebec on the platform and began to parade across it. As the camera crews scrambled to unpack their cameras, one malcontent set the Quebec flag aflame. Images of the burning fleur de lis were played and replayed on the TV screens of Quebec, enraging the residents of that province as well as many in English Canada. Only time will tell if a railway station ultimately played a decisive role in the disintegration of Canada.

That station demonstration was by no means the last. On January 15, 1990, the Tory government of Brian Mulroney eliminated half of Canada's rail passenger services. It was a move that contradicted his campaign promise to improve rail service, and one that involved changing the laws to avoid public meetings.

This postcard view is of the former Grand Trunk station at Peterborough, demolished to make way for apartment buildings.

Canada's "celebrity" station, built by the Hamilton Region Conservation Authority, and called "Sulphur Springs", has starred in TV commercials and promotions for "Anne of Green Gables" even though this Grand Trunk replica (the plans for the Grimsby, Ontario Station were used) bears no resemblance to PEI's country stations.

It also meant the end to Canada's longest-running transcontinental train service, that of the CPR.

As the last train—Train Number 1, the "Canadian"—to follow the route edged its way out of Toronto's Union Station on a frigid Sunday afternoon in January, demonstrators paraded with placards protesting the shortsightedness of their government. At stations all along the route protestors showed up with placards, banners, and coffins. At Vancouver even the Via employees joined in a mock funeral march and laying of a wreath.

But passenger train service will see a resurgence in Canada. It must, although the resurgence is unlikely to represent a return to tradition: air and road congestion, and the irresistible influence of the success of Amtrack in the U.S., will create an upswing in train travel. As it does, stations will remain a focus for many of Canada's communities, and in some ways will always be their heart and their stage.

As if to prove it, in June 1990 the Pepsi soft drink company and Toronto's popular Much Music TV channel rented a Via train that would bring Canadian youth rushing to their station, many for the first time. On June 7 the eight-car train, painted in the Pepsi colours of red, white, and blue (colours that strikingly resemble those of Amtrack), left Vancouver for stops at Jasper, Edmonton, Saskatoon, Winnipeg, Toronto, Ottawa, Montreal, Quebec City, Moncton, and Halifax. Among those on board were many of Canada's most celebrated artists such as Jeff Healey and his band, Blue Rodeo, Jane Sibbery, Paul Lane, and National Velvet. As the train stopped in front of the stations, the bands mounted a makeshift platform and

throbbed out the rock beats of the 1990s for swaying and handclapping youngsters. But it was at one of Canada's smaller communities that the largest crowds turned out. Capreol, Ontario, lies about a half hour north of Sudbury. Although a stop had not been scheduled, the organizers agreed to a request from a local Pepsi bottler and added a short stop at Capreol. Long before the train appeared down the track, more than one thousand people were milling about the station, most of them young and anxious to see their favourite Canadian music artists. An elderly couple likened the gathering to the atmosphere they remember from old-time small-town station gatherings. For indeed it was.

From the beginning Canada's stations were a stage not just for ordinary Canadians living out their daily routines, but also for writers, poets, artists, and photographers.

Poet Archibald Lampman, in his 1900 poem "The Railway Station," vividly depicts the night time arrival of a train at a small station, briefly filling the platform with the "hiss and the thunder...the faces that touch and the eyes that are dim with pain." Stephen Leacock contrasts the hustle of Union Station in Toronto with the tranquillity of his fictional "Mariposa" in his short story, "The Train to Mariposa." But perhaps Canada's most famous fictional station scene occurs on the platform of the "Bright River" station in Prince Edward Island. Matthew Cuthbert arrives to meet the "boy" that he and his sister were to adopt. Instead he finds a red-haired girl named Anne. So begins the much loved and much read *Anne of Green Gables* written by Lucy Maude Montgomery and first published in 1908.

Dr. Harry Colebourn, a Canadian army veterinarian, while on his way to Valcartier, Quebec, in 1914, disembarked onto the platform of the station in White River, Ontario, and for $20 bought a bear cub. He named his pet "Winnipeg" after his adopted home town. He could not have known that he was giving the world its best loved children's book character, Winnie the Pooh. But when he was forced to leave "Winnie" with the London Zoo in order to joint the front lines of World War I, the bear became an instant favourite of the young Christopher Robin Milne, whose father—A.A. Milne—used his son's fascination with Winnie as the basis of his enduring series of children's books. A statue has been raised in White River to celebrate the link between Winnie the Pooh and the White River station.

(right) The station platform on which Captain Colebourn bought the bear cub; (left) Winnie's tameness as demonstrated by Colebourn.

Stations appeared in a number of early paintings, such as that of Toronto's first Union station by artist William Armstrong, James Hamilton's portrayal of London's Great Western station, and W.T. Smedley's lively woodcut of Hamilton's Great Western station platform. The vanished era of steam locomotives has been captured by artist Wentworth Folkins in his series of paintings that depict steam train operations at various railway stations. Even Group of Seven artist David Milne depicted a distant silhouette of a prairie station in his 1929 painting "Railway Station." Famed artist William Kurelek captured the fear of new arrivals to the Canadian west with his painting entitled "They Sought a New World" prepared for his book *Jewish Life in Canada*. This evocative work depicts a group of turn-of-the-century Jewish immigrants huddled on the platform of a tiny and lonely prairie station.

With the overwhelming popularity of recreational train travel between 1890 and 1914, postcards were produced by the millions as souvenirs of Canada's railway stations. By 1914 Canadians had sent or received more than 60,000,000 postcards, many of them showing stations.

Some chance encounters on Canadian station platforms have had a very significant effect on world literature. Had a young Englishman named Archie Belaney not impulsively hopped off the train at Temagami, Ontario, and happened to meet woodsman Bill Guppy, he might never have been introduced to the life of Canada's natives. And the world might never have come to know "Chief" Grey Owl who claimed to be part Sioux and who went on to become a leading writer and lecturer on animal conservation. Only after his death in 1938 did a shocked world discover that Grey Owl was no Indian at all, but Belaney.

Many of Canada's surviving stations have attracted producers of movies, television shows, and commercials. Ontario's Gravenhurst station appears in "Boy in Blue," the life of rower Ned Hanlon; the Avonlea station in Saskatchewan substitutes for the demolished Wilcox station in "The Hounds of Notre Dame" (1980); while the Esquimalt and Nanaimo station at Parkesville, B.C., became the turn of the century "Kamloops" station for the climax of the movie version of the story of train robber Bill Miner, "The Grey Fox" (1983). Union Station in Toronto has substituted for a number of U.S. stations including the Chicago station in the movie "The Silver Streak" starring Gene Wilder and Richard Prior. Here the station is the victim of a runaway train that crashes through the wall.

Union Station also portrayed itself in Murray Brattle's 1974 short film "Union Station," a sensitive tribute that depicted the grandeur and many moods of the building. It was a film that, along with the book *The Open Gate*, helped save the station from demolition.

A replica of the Grimsby, Ontario, station built in 1978 by the Hamilton Region Conservation Authority in its Spring Creek Conservation Area has become Canada's star station,

popular for commercials and such films as "Mark Twain and Me," "Beautiful Dreamers," and "Anne of Green Gables." This popularity is due to the faithful attention to detail that went into the construction and to the fact that the station is not part of an operating railway.

The loss of Canadian stations has led to a sudden surge in Canadian station portraits. Stations now appear on calendars, collectors plates, and even postage stamps and lapel pins. The renewed interest, however, is mainly a lament for the past, for many of the stations have gone forever. It is often only in our books, our films, and our art that they live on.

The last crowds to come down to the station were those to watch it razed. While stations like West Toronto and Arnprior were

demolished secretly in the middle of the night, most were routinely reduced to rubble during a few short working hours. Many spectators watched with tear-reddened eyes, some remembering the excitement of past crowds and the sights, sounds, and sentiments of the station's heyday that would never be repeated. The station would have no like again. The heart of the community was gone. The stage was bare.

The CN's historic Railway Museum Train pulls into Aurora, Ontario in May, 1953.

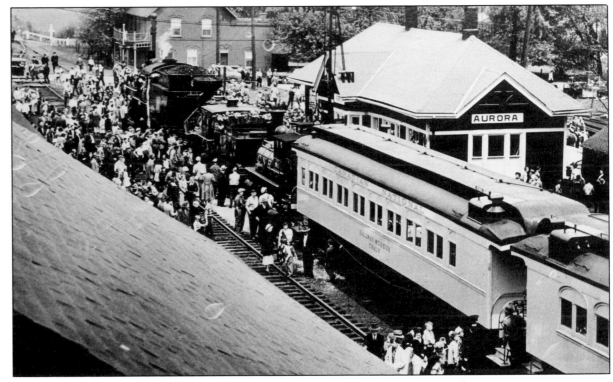

"The Train Doesn't Stop Here Any More":
Decline of the Train Station in Canada

CP Corporate Archives A 11436

The station at Rogers Pass; it was at Rogers Pass that the Trans Canada Highway was formally opened in 1962.

On June 7, 1939, at St. Catharines, Ontario, Queen Elizabeth, queen consort of King George VI, stepped into the late spring sunshine and opened the Queen Elizabeth Way, in a ceremony that symbolically commenced the demise of Canada's railway stations. The new four-lane road was the latest in superhighway design. With its controlled access and clover-leaf intersections, it was the first of its kind in North America (the Pennsylvania Turnpike would not even be started until the year after) and was a concept that would free the personal automobile from stop signs, congestion, and multiple accesses. It heralded a new era in transportation, the superhighway, and the decline of Canada's stations.

But some stations were in decline long before that. While Canada's rail era was still in its infancy wood-burning steam engines were replaced by coal-burning. These larger engines could pull longer trains and travel further before refuelling. Suddenly stations were no longer needed to provide wood at frequent intervals. And so, by 1880, before most of Canada's railway network was in place, stations had lost one of their earliest functions.

At this time Canada's railway network was expanding rapidly, with nearly one hundred separately chartered railway lines. Then two giants slowly began to emerge. Between 1890 and 1920 the CPR and the Grand Trunk began to consume the many smaller lines, through direct purchase or 999-year leases.

Within that huge spider's web the two giant corporations discovered they possessed duplicate lines, lines that had once been fierce rivals. The CPR, for example, after it had taken over the Credit Valley Line and the Toronto Grey and Bruce, had two lines that ran nearly side by side from Toronto to Orangeville. As a result, in 1932 the CPR abandoned the TG and B

line south of Orangeville and removed the tracks and the stations.

With coordination of service and elimination of duplication, fewer trains puffed along the separate lines. The trains that appeared were longer and less frequent. Redundant lines were lifted, while on the lines that remained, stations were downgraded from operator to flag stations and agents demoted to caretakers.

The 1920s and 1930s nevertheless remained the heyday of Canada's stations. More branch lines were built, and along them new stations with new styles. In the late 1920s the CPR timetables listed nearly twenty-four hundred stations, while the CNR network boasted nearly four thousand.

The Second World War witnessed a tremendous upsurge in rail travel. Soldiers, sailors, and air force pilots crammed onto troop trains to and from the Atlantic ports where ships waited to carry them to the war. The CPR alone saw passenger travel jump from seven million a year just before the war to seventeen million in 1943.

Throughout the 1950s train travel remained highly popular. The CPR introduced its passenger train, the "Canadian," and the CNR countered with its "Supercontinental." However, the clouds that would ultimately doom rail travel and eliminate nearly all of Canada's stations were forming. Dieselization, the rush of passengers from the train to the car, automatic signalling, and the end of mail and local freight service combined to end Canada's station era.

For decades the use of diesel to power locomotives had been regarded as superior to the use of coal. Diesel trains could travel half the continent before refuelling. The first diesel locomotive in Canada was built by the CNR in 1929. The major change-over from steam did not start until the late 1940s, but by 1960 diesel/electric power had completely replaced steam power. Water tanks were dismantled and coal docks sold for scrap. Many divisional stations became redundant and were downgraded or closed.

The years that followed the First World War marked another rush of innovations that further diminished the role of Canada's stations. Block signalling and centralized traffic control (CTC) began to replace the telegraph and the train order. With block signalling, the train itself tripped a switch that automatically changed the train signals and alerted the dispatcher as to its whereabouts. CTC eliminated the role of the station operator altogether, for under this revolutionary new system all train

180

(left) Although much of the line has been removed, these Credit Valley coaches await restoration by the South Simcoe Railway Society.

(right) A once busy terminus and rail link between New Brunswick and Prince Edward Island, the station and yard at Cape Tormentine lie silent.

movement was coordinated by a central dispatcher. On his board at a large central location he would watch the train movements and push a button to regulate train speeds and meets. But because of the enormous cost involved in changing the signals along thousands of miles of track, these new methods were implemented only slowly.

Following dieselization, CTC was extended along most of Canada's main railway lines. Agents and operators were removed, and stations no longer needed for maintenance crews or as passenger shelters were demolished.

Traffic control will be further streamlined when a system known as ATCS (advanced train control system) is inaugurated. Still in the experimental stage (CN was the first railway in North America to try it), ATCS will establish computer

contact with the engine cab and will electronically control all speeds and meets.

But it was the spectacular popularity of the private car and the subsequent growth of highways like the Queen Elizabeth Way that would draw Canadians away from the trains and doom most surviving stations. In 1908 Henry Ford opened his model T assembly line, and within ten years two hundred thousand cars were chugging and sputtering along Canada's muddy roads. Most of that traffic, however, was within urban areas; inter-urban travel was still difficult. It took, for example, eleven hours to travel from Toronto to Walkerton, a trip that was less than four by train and is less than two today, but by car only.

But Canada's new car owners were a deter-

mined lot. "Good Roads" associations began popping up even before the turn of the century, and in July 1901 A.W. Campbell, an Ontario provincial instructor in roadmaking, launched a "good roads" train. For fourteen weeks he drew crowds to their local station to see road-making machinery built by the Sawyer Massey Company of Hamilton, as well as cement, a relatively new product at that time, from the Canada Portland Cement Company in Deseronto.

After the First World War ended, work began on inter-urban roads. Ontario and Quebec both established government departments to build and maintain highways. Between 1920 and 1930 Canada added more than a million cars to its highways, and governments spent ninety-three million dollars to build more. This prompted Dr. Manion, then minister of railways, to criticize the use of taxes paid by railways for the construction of highways that would give an advantage to its competitors such as trucks and buses.

During the 1930s the federal government, as a depression era make-work project, assisted the provinces to construct "trunk" roads and marked the beginning of the Trans-Canada Highway. Then in 1949 the federal government passed the Trans-Canada Highway Act, legislation under which the federal government subsidized fifty per cent of the provinces' construction costs to build this new national link. In 1962 at Rogers Pass the Trans-Canada Highway was formally opened. By the 1960s Canadian governments were spending one and a quarter billion dollars annually on highways. Canadians had chosen cars over trains.

Born of the auto, suburbs sprawled across the farmlands, and more and more Canadians began living farther and farther from the stations. Within a few short years stations had gone from being the heart and focus of the community to another forgotten deteriorating building.

Express bus service began rolling along the new roads, competing with the railways for inter-urban service. The CPR actually had its own bus service south of Montreal.

In 1936 C.D. Howe created Trans-Canada Airlines, and in 1942 the CPR established its own Canadian Pacific Airlines. New international airports were opened at Toronto and Montreal, and by the late 1960s luxury-laden jet aircraft carried contented Canadians coast to coast from these modern uncrowded terminals in a scant four or five hours.

In 1963 the MacPherson Royal Commission on rail passenger service in Canada urged that much of Canada's branch-line passenger service be eliminated. Jack Pickersgill, then Liberal Transport Minister, wanted to go further. He wanted rail passenger service eliminated entirely. Moderation, however, prevailed.

To the railways the writing was clearly on the wall; they began to terminate their passenger services, some say with undue haste. In arguing before the Canadian Transport Commission (CTC) in 1965 for the discontinuation of its new transcontinental train, less than ten years after it had opened to great fanfare, the CPR stated that the "continuing demonstration by the public of a marked and increasing preference for the private automobile for shorter trips and jet aircraft for longer trips, [that] there appears to be no foreseeable change in this trend...[we have] no choice but to consolidate, substitute, reduce and eliminate [rail passenger] services which have shown deterioration." Ironically, at the same time as the CPR set out these arguments the CNR was advertising the inauguration of a "Fast Railliner to Saskatoon and Prince Albert [from Regina] comfortable, fast CN Railliner service is the worry-free way to travel."

More interested in freight profits than in unprofitable passenger lines, the railways began to request the CTC's permission to close passenger service and demolish stations on branch lines, claiming they were unprofitable. Accusations that decline in passenger travel was deliberately orchestrated through inconvenient scheduling were upheld at CTC hearings into shut-down requests.

The railways were also accused of making passenger lines look unprofitable by assigning shared passenger-freight costs completely against passenger revenues.

This allegation gains considerable credibility when one reviews federal costing order R

(right) Passenger service on the CPR line between Toronto and Havelock fell victim to cutbacks of "uneconomic" branch lines.

(far right) The CPR's much publicized 'Canadian' hadn't been on the rails long before the CPR wanted to reduce passenger service. Here it sits at the Golden BC station in 1966.

6313 which sets out the formula by which CN and CP can charge certain costs back to Via Rail. The order allows CN and CP to impose charges against Via for the use of their lines, equipment, and personnel that are arbitrary and unaccountable. For example, according to an allegation put forward by the Federal Liberal Task Force on Via Rail, a fuse bought by CN from Bombardier for $2.78 was later resold to Via for $48. The same report revealed that CN charges Amtrak 1/3 less for use of its track than it charges Via. The order also allows CN to charge Via for the use of its stations even though these buildings, property of a Crown corporation, belong to the people of Canada.

The government itself made decisions during the late 1980s intended to make rail passenger service still less profitable. It cancelled the purchase of bi-level passenger cars for the hugely popular summer run of the "Canadian." It also cancelled a program investigating the purchase of efficient rail buses to serve unprofitable remote centres. Finally, in 1990 during its unpopular and misguided sweeping rail passenger cuts, the federal government removed the

"Canadian" from the more heavily populated and scenic CP route to the longer, less populated, and less scenic CN route.

Although tourists booked the "Canadian" solid during the summer months, the government also reduced its run from daily to three times weekly, ignoring the main reason the daily "Canadian" appeared to lose so much money, namely that it was also run on a daily schedule during the "dead" winter season.

It is little wonder that Canada's dwindling rail passenger service appears so unprofitable. From the all-time high of 55.4 million passengers carried in 1945, ridership had plummeted to 27.2 million by the mid-1950s. By 1970 most of Canada's branch-line passenger service had ended. More cuts followed in 1982 and 1990 until barely 6 million Canadians were

able to use the railway.

Seen as a panacea during the Pickersgill days, the auto and the airplane have since proven to be environmental disasters. Flights were routinely backed up, while the air around airports turned orange from pollution and deafening from jet noise. Meanwhile, cars and trucks gobbled up increasing amounts of fossil fuels turning urban traffic into a chocking nightmare of gridlock and exhaust fumes.

However, Ottawa's transportation planners remained mired in the 1960s and continued to turn a blind eye to rail. In a so-called environmental analysis on his proposed Via Rail cuts released by Tory Transportation Minister Benoit Bouchard in 1989 the effects of exhaust fumes from increased auto use were completely ignored.

But cuts to passenger service were not alone responsible for the decline in stations. The railways continued to offer commercial telegraph service through CN/CP Telecommunications long after the telegraph ended any relevance it had to railway operation. Once telephones had become a feature in every home, the telegraph service was removed from the station and was operated centrally.

With the dramatic decline in passenger traffic after World War II and the elimination of passenger service on many routes, station functions were reduced to that of handling freight. Cattle, crops, timber, and factory products kept many stations open. But the competition from trucks loomed ominously on the horizon. In 1948 the first freight truck rumbled along the Trans-Canada Highway between Fort William

Following the 1990 cutbacks, VIA coaches sit on sidings at the Ottawa station awaiting shipment to Mexico.

and Winnipeg, breaking the CPR's long-standing freight monopoly. In 1950 a nine-day railway strike drove shippers to willing truckers, and many never returned to the railways.

The central carload concept was introduced in 1960 by the New York Central Railway. They touted it as "a revolutionary departure from the old fashioned horse-and-buggy method of railway freight agency service." The new method featured travelling representatives who replaced the agent with pick-up and delivery by truck at the plant or factory which then moved the goods to and from a distant central facility. The new process eliminated the need for the local station agents to involve themselves in freight handling, once one of their main tasks. Now everything was done by truck and toll-free telephone.

By the mid-1970s fewer than one station in fifteen generated enough revenue to cover costs. Even though agents were paid for full eight-hour shifts, some stations were experiencing less than fifteen minutes' worth of business per day. To halt this tremendous inefficiency

the Canadian railways, following the U.S. example, ended one of Canada's longest railway traditions, local freight service, replacing it with piggybacking and containerization. Instead of booking through a local station agent, shippers would deal by telephone through a central or regional carload centre.

Trucks sped off along multi-lane highways carrying products that had until then been shipped from the local way station directly to massive railway yards. At those yards the trailer or the container was hoisted directly onto the railway car and shipped on unit trains to a similar cental yard near the destination, where trucks would again take over. (Piggy-backing was nothing new to railways. In 1855 Joseph Howe instituted a form of piggybacking on Nova Scotia short lines where farmers' wagons were hoisted onto flatcars for the trip to their destination.)

With the advent of containerization and piggybacking, stations by the hundreds were deprived of their last community function, and closed their doors forever. By the 1970s most

stations had lost their functions entirely; mail, signalling, and freight, all disappeared. Only along those few lines that still offered passenger service were stations left up, paint peeling and windows broken, to provide shelter for waiting passengers. Unmaintained, these rambling old buildings became expensive to maintain and sometimes impossible to insure. They were often bulldozed into rubble and replaced with small shelters in which waiting passengers might huddle against the cold.

The death of the Forward, Saskatchewan, station is typical. Although the drought and depression combined to eliminate hundreds of full-time station agents during the 1930s, few stations were closed. Only where revenue was very small was closure proposed, as in the case of Forward. Once a busy farm town with both CN and CP stations, by the 1930s Forward had become a virtual ghost town and CN wanted to close the station. The local reaction was immediate and loud. "There will be no service for people between Radville and Forward," roared the rural council, "it is the people of these districts whose wheat going from prairie farm to the Atlantic that contributes to keeping these stations open."

But the Board of Railway Commissioners was sceptical. "There were only 27 tons shipped out [of Forward] with revenue of $234," commented the local inspector. "I am very familiar with this territory and for the past 4 or 5 years it has become almost a desert." The commission approved downgrading of the agency to caretaker status. By 1962 revenue from Forward had vanished along with its population. In 1963 the station was finally removed. Today the site of this once bustling spot is an overgrown field. Even the former railway bed is barely discernible.

The 1960s witnessed the first wave of wholesale station demolition. Of more than 270 stations that stood on the dense network of lines through Quebec's eastern townships, fewer than 25 survived the decade. Between April and July 1975 the CNR applied to the CTC for permission to demolish nearly 100 stations in Saskatchewan alone. In 1979–80 that province lost another 100 stations. On August 9, 1974, the CTC agreed to allow the CNR to demolish 50 stations in Manitoba. Between 1970 and 1980 railways in Ontario were given permission to remove more than 140 stations. In 1979 the CNR announced to Newfoundlanders that 29 of their stations were to be closed and 14 agents made redundant.

In a 1970 *Toronto Star* article Tom Ford observed that "Toronto is gobbling up industry at the expense of Ontario's small towns. As a result the CNR wants to close 350 country stations where it is losing business."

Towns that depended heavily or solely upon the station and the business that it generated were often reduced to ghost towns. The remote rockland of northern Ontario was particularly hard hit, for many of the towns there were built solely to support the railway. One-time divisional towns like Reddit, Foleyet, and Nakina, remote and surrounded by miles of silent bushland, contain only maintenance or way crews. The roundhouses have been demolished, the maintenance shops are mere foundations. The stores and hotels have closed, and many residents have moved away. The massive station at Reddit was torn down in the 1970s, that at Foleyet in 1990, and that at Nakina has been saved, for the moment, by the town.

Across the prairies, towns closed down by the hundreds, and today Canadians can find ghost towns literally every eight miles simply by following the abandoned branch lines.

In just two short decades the railway stations of Canada had gone from being the most important institution in town to the status of a hole in the ground, their many vital functions becoming fast-fading memories to the millions to whom they had been the heart of the community.

The old railway hotel and main street at Maleval, Saskatchewan, fell victim to the abandonment of the railway line that once ran through the busy town.

The demolition of the CPR's Tudoresque West
Toronto station started a concerted national
effort to rescue surviving stations.

"Boarded-up Shacks":
The Fight to Save Our Stations

"Just a boarded-up shack," was how CP law-
yer Donald Maxwell dismissed the West
Toronto Station before three Federal
Court judges as he tried to justify the CPR's
pre-dawn demolition of the building.

In 1979 the CPR closed the station and
told anyone who cared to listen that they
wanted to tear it down. But the station, a
large Tudor revival building , had been a
West Toronto landmark since it was built in
1912, and residents and politicians alike
were determined that it should stay.

Station closings had become rampant dur-

ing the 1970s in both the U.S. and Canada, and
a variety of alternative uses were being found for
them. Libraries, museums, seniors' drop-in centres, municipal offices, and private-sector activities could all be housed in redundant stations,
usually without moving the building. Some railway companies, the CPR among them, insisted
that stations must be moved.

The preservationists, however, were hop-
ing to change the CPR's mind about the West
Toronto Station. The City of Toronto, the
West Toronto Historical Society, and the CPR
had been conducting a feasibility study into

turning the building into a farmers' market, but after four years of talking the CPR had had enough. During the pre-dawn hours of November, 1982, a CPR wrecking crew quietly fenced off the site and began to demolish. By the time the city awoke the station was rubble. Toronto mayor Arthur Eggleton, furious, rushed to the scene and handed the crew orders to stop work. They refused. It was too late anyhow.

Denounced as "corporate vandalism" and likened to a "commando raid," the West Toronto demolition made headlines across the country. But it also struck a responsive note. Too many Canadians had stood by, teary eyed and enraged, as they watched their stations fall under the bulldozer's blade.

Among these were the residents of Renfrew, Pembroke, Almonte, and Arnprior. In 1982 these Ottawa Valley towns had pleaded with the CPR to save their magnificent stone stations. Built of local limestone to a special architectural plan, these stations were unlike any other in Canada. In all cases the CPR told the communities that the stations must be moved. But the costs of moving the large stone structures would have exceeded one hundred and fifty thousand dollars, more than small communities could afford.

Meanwhile the CNR wrecking crews were busily knocking down the ancient stone stations between Toronto and Montreal, the original stations built by the Grand Trunk Railway in the mid-1850s, as well as the Maritimes' eclectic collection of stations built by the Intercolonial Railway. Many of the them were over 120 years old and were among the oldest stations in Canada.

In some cases municipalities themselves were to blame for losing stations. Offered the opportunity to preserve its station, a rare exam-

The Nipigon Ontario station once dominated its main street; it became a victim of the times. The frame CPR station in this northern Ontario railway town was its most prominent building. Since 1928 it had stood grandly on the main street opposite the town's four blocks of stores. Carefully tended lawns and gardens stretched away on either side. When the CPR told the town of its intentions to demolish the station, the residents agreed to move it. Although the twenty-thousand-dollar price tag for the move was steep for a town of just two thousand, the determined residents raised the amount. Then just two days before the move, CP advised them that they would need eight thousand dollars more to remove the signal arm, and thirty thousand more for rewiring. The coffers were dry and, although the CPR had itself contributed to the fund, the people of Nipigon could not come up with another cent. The CPR demolished the station.

Streetsville's original Credit Valley station is now a house. In the early 1900s, when the CPR was replacing many of the old stations that it had inherited from the Credit Valley Railway, two of these intriguing turreted stations, at Milton and at Streetsville, were moved away to become houses, and yet survive. The station that replaced that structure was not to be so fortunate. In 1982 the CPR declared its intention to demolish its 1914 station and replace it with an aluminum prefab. The citizens of Streetsville joined with the provincial government to try to prevent the removal of the old brick station. Using economic arguments, they pointed to a cost study showing that the CPR would save sixty thousand dollars if it upgraded the station instead of replacing it. The CPR announced that it was not in the heritage business, and the station came down.

Down comes the Port Arthur CPR station to make way for road widening.

(right) The town of Kapuskasing rallied to save its station. The town bought the station and today successfully operates out of it a travel agency and bus depot. Train service to the Kapuskasing station was suspended only in 1990 with the Tory government's infamous rail passenger cuts.

(far right) The Glencoe station in southwestern Ontario.

ple of an early Canadian National style complete with original wood shingle exterior and board platform, the town of Smooth Rock Falls, Ontario, declined. The station is now gone.

In other cases the railway insisted upon conditions that are simply too unreasonable for the municipality to accept. When the CN offered the Glencoe station, a rare example of a turreted frame Grand Trunk station, to the town, council found CN's conditions too onerous.

Station demolition is nothing new in Canada. As communities grew, small stations were replaced with larger ones; older buildings deteriorated and were replaced with buildings that were sounder and warmer. But stations were always there.

Canada's early station recycling had little to do with heritage preservation. It was simply a practical way to acquire a cheap building. The first recorded station to be recycled was the Great Western station in Toronto. Built in 1856, it was abandoned in 1872 when the new union station was opened. It survived as a farmers' market until 1952, when it burned down.

One of the more impressive recycling examples occurred on the former Bay of Quinte Rail-

way in central Ontario. When the line was abandoned in 1942, nearly every station between the villages of Queensborough and Newburgh, six in all, was preserved. These solid two-storey stuccoed stations all survive on site, all but one a private house, and all retain their original appearance, including freight sheds, trademark narrow cement platforms, and unusual two-storey bay windows.

One of the first stations to be preserved for its heritage value was that at Petrolia, Ontario. By the 1930s the oil boom that had fuelled the town's prosperity and had inspired the Grand Trunk to build a twin-towered brick station on the main street, had gone sour; the station was closed. Recognizing the heritage value of the building, the town acquired the station for its library. The former ticket office became the librarian's office, the baggage room the children's library, and the ladies' waiting room the library boardroom.

After the Second World War and, more particularly, in the 1960s, Canadians began to realize that their stations were going for good. By then most functions had gone; passenger lines had been closed, computers had replaced the

(above) Designed by the firm of Ross and MacFarlane, Ottawa's Central Station (later Union Station) was part of the beaux arts wave that swept North American station building. Passengers entered a high-ceilinged waiting room through classical columns that stretched four storeys high. The station is now a conference hall; its converted waiting room witnessed the Meech Lake fiasco of 1990. Unfortunately, the public may see only the exterior. Uniformed security guards sternly prohibit unauthorized persons from viewing the former grand waiting hall and concourse.

(right) Manitoba's Miami station is now a drop in centre for seniors.

telegraph, local freight had been bumped by containerization, and the mail had been given over to the airlines.

Another post-war craze was urban renewal. During the 1960s planners and politicians felt that the solution to downtown deterioration was demolition. Low-cost houses were targeted as "slums" and bulldozed; fine old commercial buildings were replaced with faceless blocks of glass and concrete.

The urban renewalists then turned to inner-city railway tracks. Regarded as unsightly and a nuisance, many downtown tracks were removed. Newer stations, designed to look more like airport terminals, were relegated to the suburbs within easier reach of the car-driving public. In Saskatoon and Oshawa, when new stations opened in the suburbs during the 1960s their historic downtown predecessors were demolished. The citizens of Saint John, N.B., lost their solid neo-classical station to an uninteresting glass station in the 1970s. The surrounding land, cleared for the anticipated urban growth, remains vacant. In the 1960s plans to beautify Ottawa called for the removal of all downtown railway tracks. A new

station opened further out, and the historic union station was threatened with removal. Ottawa, however, has long prided itself on its heritage, and the station was preserved as a conference hall.

Heritage also won the day in Quebec City. The preoccupation with suburbia and the nuisance of several level train crossings led to the removal of rail passenger service from the old Gare du Palais in 1976 to a newer suburban station in Ste Foy. With the subsequent removal of freight traffic in the core area, passenger train movement began to be perceived as less of a problem. In 1985 Via Rail and the City of Quebec pumped twenty-eight million dollars into restoring the magnificent chateauesque building, and passenger trains rumbled in once more. It was a rare example of a train station being recycled as a train station.

Almost as if to negate this expense and effort, the Conservative government of Canada in 1990 ordered that all passenger trains be re-routed off the more direct and more populated CP tracks that connected Quebec with Montreal along the north shore, and onto the longer and less populated south-shore CN trackage.

After having for generations taken their stations for granted, Canadians began to value stations for their architectural merit, for the vital role they played in the community, and simply for nostalgia, and they became more active in saving them.

Stations by the hundreds were being dragged off to become homes, cottages, and chicken coops. Others were being plunked down in museum grounds, sandwiched inappropriately between pioneer log cabins and pioneer churches. Despite the interest, few were being saved as "stations," and fewer still on their original site.

On the prairies when branch-line abandonment and station demolition became rampant during the mid-1970s, most communities were more concerned with the closure of elevators and factories and the loss of jobs than they were with the loss of station buildings. But the concern over stations was not far behind.

Communities rallied to find ways of saving them. Many became museums, such as those at High River, Alberta; Frenchman's Butte, Saskatchewan; and Avonlea, Saskatchewan. Manitoba's Miami station became a senior citizens' drop-in centre. These stations were all preserved on site.

When the CNR abandoned most of its railway operations on Prince Edward Island in the 1980s, many stations were still around. Some ended up simply as farm storage buildings. Others became garages, stores, houses, or restaurants. Four of the architecturally more pleasing stations, those at Montague and Elmira, and the stone stations at Alberton and Kensington, have become either museums or tourist centres. Meanwhile, the large urban terminal at Charlottetown became a farmers' market for a time.

In Nova Scotia a few stations are being re-used on site, the stations at Musquodoboit and Louisbourg as tourist centres, the fascinating station at Pictou as a community centre. On Cape Breton Island the ancient wooden Intercolonial station at Orangedale now belongs to the municipality. One of Canada's oldest on-site stations, the Rothesay, N.B., station of the former European and North American Railway (built in 1858) is an artist's studio.

In Ontario the Ontario Northland Railway not only contributed its demolition costs towards the preservation of the Cobalt, Ontario, station, but has allowed its reuse on site. An ambitious building designed by John Lyle, its grandeur reflects the long-vanished days when Cobalt was the centre of a frenzied silver boom and one of the richest and most promising towns in Canada. One of the few relics of those glory days, the station now houses a private collection of military memorabilia and offices.

CN and CP, however, required that many be moved. While smaller way stations were relatively inexpensive to move, larger stations and urban stations were prohibitively expensive to relocate and were often demolished. In many instances CP financially aided the relocation of a station, often contributing an amount equivalent to the cost of demolition.

Much, however, is lost when a station is removed from its site. For the historic role of the station was that of gateway between the community and the outside. Removed from that location, it becomes just another building and is often altered beyond recognition. Even when stations are preserved in pioneer villages or relocated to a vacant village lot on some back street, they look awkward and out of place.

Moving a station is costly and difficult. When the Canadian Railway Museum purchased the Barrington station in Quebec it paid the CN a token one dollar. Then the hard part began. The procession that hauled the station along Quebec's roads to the museum in Delston included, in addition to museum staff, the contractor's three trucks, six Bell Telephone cars, three vehicles from Quebec Hydro, one truck each from the Shawinigan and Southern power companies, and two Quebec Provincial Police vehicles, a veritable parade that included seventeen vehicles and twenty-six staff.

As with the Barrington station, relocation is more successful when a station is incorporated into a railway theme. The Bellis, Alberta, station became the centrepiece of the Ukrainian heritage village east of Edmonton. Several prairie buildings were placed along a typical prairie street. Dominating the street is the station, reflecting the role that stations played in the prairie communities. The interior of this former Canadian Northern station was accurately furnished as a turn-of-the-century station. Operator's paraphernalia clutter the office, period furniture fills the living quarters, and outside the baggage carts, boxcars, and distant grain elevators all complete the authenticity. The St. Albert station was moved to a site north of Edmonton where the Alberta Pioneer Railway Association has added a wooden water tower and runs a steam excursion along a mile of track.

History is even better served when the station remains on site and continues to play a "station" role. The former St. James Station in Winnipeg remains on its original site and is the point of departure for the popular Prairie Dog Special excursion operated by the Vintage Locomotive Society of Winnipeg. In Ontario the Smiths Falls Railway Museum Association has preserved the former Smiths Falls Canadian Northern station on the original site, where the society has established a museum and runs short excursions. Similarly, the Port Stanley and Union stations in Ontario have been restored and are the termini for the Port Stanley Terminal Railway excursions.

The PEIR station at Elmira, P.E.I., is now a railway museum complete with track and rolling stock, as is the former Newfoundland Railway station at Avondale, Newfoundland, the oldest in that province.

But despite the best intentions of concerned citizens and preservationists, much remained in the way of preserving stations. First, there were

The former CP station from Laggan (now Lake Louise), like that from Sheppard, Alberta, was moved to Heritage Park in Calgary; the two stations now relive their traditional role as the focus of the rebuilt community, and are the points of embarkation for a vintage steam train that puffs around the perimeter of the park.

(below) Workers restore the facade of the Peterborough CPR station, acquired in 1990 by the Chamber of Commerce.

(above right) When Toronto's Union Station was threatened in 1964, a station committee was formed and authors Pierre Berton, Mike Filey, and several others pooled their considerable talents to produce *The Open Gate*, edited by Richard Bedout. This is a book that probes the social, architectural, and operational history of the station and is considered one of the best books on stations ever produced. Certainly its impact in Toronto was stunning. Rather than demolishing the station, CN, Via, and the federal government pumped three million dollars into giving the station a facelift. The Great Hall, the largest room in Canada, was washed, and the Indiana limestone that made up the exterior was scraped and scrubbed clean of its five decades of smoke, soot, and gypsum. The station was not just preserved; it was born again. Although Via trains are fewer, the station is the focus for an expanding network of GO commuter trains. The commuter concourse was completely redone to allow easier access to the subway and to underground malls and office towers.

the railways. CPR's policy, and that of the CNR in many instances, was that for safety reasons the stations had to be moved. Non-railway uses, they argued, were incompatible adjacent to an operating railway and posed a threat to the public. This policy was often applied even to lightly used branch lines and lines up for abandonment.

It is, however, a rationale that cannot be substantiated. Often, once the station has been moved, the railway sells or redevelops the property into a use that could just as easily have been incorporated into the station building itself. The retention of a station on site poses no greater threat to public safety than any other reuse of a vacant station site.

The policy also ignores local zoning. Once a railway sells the station to a non-railway purchaser, municipalities can through their local zoning bylaws control the reuse of the station

and apply conditions that would set out fencing and parking requirements, and even where the public can walk. In this way the preservation of a station by a new purchaser may be safer than if the station or the land were to remain in the railway's ownership and beyond the ability of the municipality to regulate.

It is on occasion possible to sway the railway companies from this position. When the residents of Avonlea, Saskatchewan, first approached CN to sell them the station for a museum, the CN ordered it moved. Persuasion from provincial and federal politicians that the lightly used branch line posed no threat convinced the CN to allow the station to remain.

One of the more interesting battles to save stations was waged in the Laurentian Mountains north of Montreal. Passenger service along the Mont Laurier line had survived into the 1980s thanks to the popularity of the winter ski trains. As a result, when Jean Luc Pepin, Liberal minister of transport, closed passenger service in 1980, many of the original stations were still in place.

Shortly thereafter the CPR began to remove

these stations, and by 1985 nine of them had come down. That's when Adrien Gregoire, a municipal councillor and economic development officer in Annonciation, went to work. Recognizing the historic and economic benefit of saving the old stations, he rallied other municipalities along the line to pressure the CPR to hold back the wrecking crews. In 1987 the CPR agreed to allow the municipalities to take them over.

It was not just small towns that faced the loss of their stations. In 1964 the president of CN threatened to demolish what is considered one of the most magnificent stations in North America, Toronto's Union Station. The controversial Metro Centre plan proposed levelling the existing structure and replacing it with several office towers. Toronto rallied; Union Station has now once more become the focus of the downtown.

In 1973 Canada's other grand old station, CPR's Windsor Station in Montreal, was threatened with demolition. As in Toronto, Montrealers formed a committee to save the station and convinced the CPR to preserve the historic structure. Instead of tearing it down, the

CPR poured eighteen million dollars into its restoration. And so the words that William Van Horne placed on a six-foot sign a century ago when he opened the station apply once again today: "Beats all creation, the new CPR station."

As with Union and Windsor stations, many redundant and tattered old stations have been revived as commuter stations. The Quebec minister of transport has spent two million dollars to alter former CP stations at Beaconsfield, Vaudreuil, Montreal Ouest, and Valois for use by commuters. Improvements have included new platforms, period lighting, pedestrian tunnels, and building restoration. All stations were built in the early years of the twentieth century. The handsome old buildings at Hudson and Rigaud also remain as commuter waiting rooms. Sadly, however, the original CPR station at Dorval, much loved by railway photographers from across North Amer-

ica, was demolished just before it could celebrate its one hundredth birthday.

GO Transit, Ontario's commuter railway, has recently completed feasibility studies to preserve the historic former Grand Trunk stations at Maple, Bradford, and Aurora. The former Grand Trunk stations in Brampton and Georgetown have been used by GO for several years.

Via Rail has also been active in preserving stations. It now owns or leases many former CN and CP stations and wants to present the best possible face to attract travellers. In 1987 the company spent $11.5 million in restoration and renovations to stations, in 1988 a further $13.7 million. Among its achievements were the facelifting of Toronto's Union Station, the reactivation of Quebec's Gare du Palais, and the restoration of the Levis station. It has paid attention to such details as benches and ticket counters in the Trois Rivières station, the

stained glass windows in the Gare du Palais, and the doors, windows, and counters in the Halifax station.

Such success was far from universal. Commuters along a popular CP line between Toronto and Peterborough fixed up and repainted the several old "Van Horne" stations that lined their route. The buildings, however, remained the property of the CPR; between 1978 and 1983 the railway, which no longer needed them, demolished all but two.

But it was the West Toronto demolition that awoke Canadians to the realization that the whole country was rapidly losing a vital component of its heritage. No longer would stations remain a local issue. The problem lay not just with the railway companies that considered the stations to be "shacks," but with a loophole in federal/provincial heritage laws. Simply put, stations could not legally be preserved. Rail-

ways had only to apply to the Canadian Transportation Committee for approval to demolish. The CTC had no mandate to consider heritage factors. In hearings to consider a CPR demolition application, five of thirteen witnesses presented heritage-related arguments, but the CTC dismissed them all in a single sentence.

Under the federal-provincial division of power, only the provinces are allowed to designate buildings for heritage protection. However, because railways are federally regulated, provincial heritage legislation can't touch them. Even though most provinces, Ontario excepted, have legislation that permits the provincial minister to designate and preserve historical buildings, railway stations remained exempt.

Only where the railways agreed to a designation could the provinces act. In Saskatchewan twenty-five CN stations have been designated with the concurrence of the railway, nearly all on lightly used or subsequently abandoned branch lines. Although the Newfoundland Railway has now been abandoned, two of its stations, those at Avondale and Carbonnear, have both been designated as heritage structures and have been allocated ten thousand dollars each from the Heritage Foundation of Newfoundland and Labrador for exterior restoration.

This was not, however, possible in Ontario. The Ontario Heritage Act, described as one of the weakest in the western world, places the entire onus to preserve buildings upon the municipalities, and then makes the preconditions so cumbersome that only the largest and most sophisticated have the resources to do so. Stranger still, the act denies the province itself the power to designate structures of wider his-

(left) Kingston's former K and P station, now a tourist information centre, fits right into the town's stone heritage.

(above) The CPR has allowed its London, Ontario, station to be incorporated into a private development.

torical significance.

In other respects, however, Ontario has led the fight to preserve stations. The Ministry of Culture and Communications has published kits that advise municipalities what strategies and techniques they might use to save their stations. The kit contains historical and architectural information on Ontario's railway networks and its stations. It provides users with legal information and how SOS (Save Our Station) committees might be organized.

A program initiated by Ontario's Ministry of Transportation helps finance the preservation of railway stations as intermodal terminals. In partnership with local municipalities, the ministry will fund up to seventy-five per cent of the analytical and capital costs. The aim is to provide train/bus terminals operated by the municipalities with commercial space to help offset

operating costs. At the time of writing, stations at Gravenhurst, Orillia, and St. Mary's have been preserved under this program.

Another Ontario agency involved in station preservation is the non-profit Ontario Heritage Foundation. One of its notable successes was the restoration of the 1856 Grand Trunk station in Port Hope, Ontario. That agency, along with CN, Via Rail, and the town, contributed $180,000 to fully restore the station. The work involved replacing the exterior limestone and restoring the interior for both CN railway crew and Via passengers. Built in the classical five-arch stone Grand Trunk style of the 1850s, Port Hope's is the oldest functioning railway station in Canada. The OHF has also assisted with the recycling of the CP station at Peterborough and the ONR station at Cobalt.

Despite all provincial efforts, the greatest hurdle remained the federal law. While exempting railways from all provincial laws, federal legislation makes no provision for history. Even though the National Historic Sites and Monuments Act allows stations to be designated as national historic sites, that act makes no provision to preserve them. (In Ottawa a historical convent was demolished the day after it had been designated a national historic site.) Although stations at Prescott, St. Mary's Junction (both in Ontario), and Macadam (New Brunswick) are national historic sites, the railways may still legally demolish them.

Spurred on by the West Toronto demolition, the Heritage Canada Foundation, led by its Ottawa director, Jacques Dalibard, was determined to finally plug the loophole. In 1983 the foundation enlisted Liberal MP Jesse Flis to introduce Bill C-253, a private member's bill "to protect heritage railway stations." But the bill was plagued by delays. In 1984 an election left it on the order paper, and again in 1986 parliament prorogued before the bill had been through committee. Its prospects appeared more encouraging when it was introduced for the third time in 1986. Thanks largely to heavy lobbying by Heritage Canada, and to the angry mood of the nation following CP's conviction in 1987 (later overturned) of criminal charges over its West Toronto demolition, the bill drew overwhelming support from MPs of all parties and from Tom MacMillan, minister of the environment. It passed in the Commons unanimously.

But in the Senate it ran into more hurdles. One of them was Liberal senator Ian Sinclair, who six years earlier as head of CP Rail had "for the good of the people," as he put it, ordered the demolition of the West Toronto Station. Sinclair along with his Liberal colleagues began to place a variety of procedural obstacles in the way of the bill, including referrals to committees and skirmishes over the wording of the French text. But the public reaction against their tactics was so overwhelming that one by one the Liberal senators backed off. Finally, on September 21 when the vote was taken, the only senator to oppose the railway station preservation bill was the man who demolished West Toronto, Ian Sinclair.

The Heritage Railway Station Protection Act heralded a new dawn for station preservation, at least for those that remain. Under the new law, once a station is given a heritage designation the railway company may neither demolish it nor alter it. To place a station upon the protected list any province, municipality, or individual may recommend to the Historical Sites and Monuments Board the station they want preserved. The board evaluates the historical, architectural, and environmental significance of the station and may then recommend it to the minister of the environment for protection.

When the legislation was proclaimed, twelve stations appeared on the list: the CNR Smithers station in B.C., CPR's Lake Louise and Red Deer stations in Alberta, the CN and CP stations in Winnipeg, as well as CN Dauphin and CP Virden. In Ontario the list includes the CN stations in Aurora and Brantford, the former Canada Southern station in St. Thomas, and Union Station in Toronto. In eastern Canada only CP's Windsor Station in Montreal was initially protected.

Although this legislation places Canada in the forefront of station preservation (in the U.S. even being placed on the National Historic Register does not guarantee preservation), problems remain. Most of the stations on the initial list are in no immediate danger of demolition. Other stations, in more immediate danger, are omitted.

The second problem is the length of time needed for a station to be chosen. Only a limited number are reviewed at one time, and even then it takes at least another year to make the protected list. The railway demolition crews don't take that long to demolish a station.

The third problem remains what to do with a redundant station once it is on the list. Designation still does not guarantee that a new use will be found for it. Many stations may literally fall apart while awaiting a new owner.

There are, however, some glimmers of hope that the railway companies themselves are beginning to understand the importance of their heritage to Canadians. In London, Ontario, the CPR has allowed its turn-of-the-century station to be incorporated into a redevelopment proposal as a restaurant. The 1916 North Toronto, or Summerhill, Station has become the centrepiece for Marathon Realty's plans to redevelop its lands around the building.

The fight to save Canada's stations is far from over. There have been victories, and far too many losses, but at least there is the awareness that stations are part of a heritage that goes far beyond the style of the building or its size, or even beyond the specific role it played in a particular community. The station was much more. It was the gateway for many newly arriving Canadians, its was the social heart of small-town Canada, and it was the door through which immigrants entered to seek new life in a new land, as well as the door through which many Canadians left their homes, some never to return. It was part and parcel of the creation of this land, a symbol of a nation. The station may be a thing of the past, for the most part, but it is a past that should never be forgotten, even though the train doesn't stop there any more.

BIBLIOGRAPHY

Alexander, Edwin P. *Down at the Depot, American Railroad Stations From 1831 to 1920*, Clarkson N. Potter, New York, 1970.

Allaby, Ian. "GO Transit Moves a City," *Canadian Geographic*, December, 1988.

Anderson, Allan and Betty Tomlinson. *Greetings From Canada; An Album of Unique Canadian Postcards of the Edwardian Era 1900 to 1916*, MacMillan, Toronto, 1978.

Andreae, Christopher. *Railway Heritage study in Toronto*.

Andreae, Christopher. *A Historical Railway Atlas of Southwestern Ontario*, C.A. Andreae, London, 1972.

Andreae, Christopher. *The Story of the London-Port Stanley Railway*, Gage, Toronto, 1986.

Archibald, William. 'All Aboard the "Y" Train', *Canadian National Magazine*, October 1956.

Annual Reports, various. Board of Railway Commissioners.

Artibise, F.J. *Prairie Urban Development* Canadian Historical Association, Booklet #34, Ottawa, 1981.

Ashdown, Dana. *Railway Steamships of Ontario*, Boston Mills Press, Erin, 1988.

Backhouse, Frances. 'Glacier House: A Loving Look at a Lost Lifestyle' *Canadian Geographic*, August/September, 1987.

'Bag and Baggage'. *CP Staff Bulletin*, January, 1944, reprinted in *Canadian Rail*, 402, January/Febuary, 1988.

Baird, Ian. *Canadian Pacific Railway Stations in British Columbia*, ORCA Book Publishers, Victoria BC, 1990.

Baird, Ian. *A Historical Guide to the E and N Railway*, Victoria BC, Heritage Architectural Guide, 1985.

Barnes, Michael. *Link With a Lonely Land: the Temiskaming and Northern Ontario Railway*, Boston Mills Press, 1985.

Barr, Elinor, and Betty Dyok. *Ignace: A Saga of the Shield*, Prairie Publishing Co. Winnipeg, 1979.

Bedbrook, W.J. 'The New Look in Railway Stations', *Canadian Rail*.

Bedout, R., ed., with John Taylor and Mike Filey. *The Open Gate: Toronto Union Station*, Peter Martin Assoc., Toronto, 1972.

Bennett, Carol, and D.W. McCuaig. *In Search of the K and P.*, Renfrew Advance, Renfrew Ontario, 1981.

Berton, Pierre. *The Great Railway*, McClelland and Stewart, Toronto, 1972.

Bohi, Charles. *Canadian National's Western Depots*, Railfare Enterprises, Toronto, 1977.

Bohi, Charles. 'Country Depots in Saskatchewan', *Canadian Rail*, September/October, 1988.

Bohi, Charles and H.R. Grant. 'Standardized Railroad Stations of Saskatchewan' *Saskatchewan History*, Vol XXXI, Autumn, 1978.

Bohi, Charles and L.S. Kozma. *Canadian Pacific in Alberta and Saskatchewan*, British Railway Modellers of North America, Calgary, 1987.

Bond, Courtney C.J. *City on the Ottawa: A Detailed Historical Guide to Ottawa*, Queens Printer, Ottawa, 1961.

Booth, J. Derek. *Railways of Southern Quebec*, Railfare, Toronto, 1982, 2 vols.

Booth, J. Derek. 'Railway Stations in Southern Quebec', *Canadian Rail*, 256, April, 1973.

Bouchier, M.F. 'The Impact of the Northern Railroad on the Sense of Place in Canada West, 1850-65', M.A. Thesis, York University, 1979.

Bousfield, A., and G. Teffoli. *Royal Spring*, Dundurn Press, Toronto, 1989.

Bowers, Peter. *Two Divisions to Bluewater*, Boston Mills Press, Erin, 1983.

Boyer, B.A. *Muskoka's Grand Hotels*, Boston Mills Press, Erin, 1987.

Brault, Lucien. *The Mile of History*, National Capital Commission, Ottawa, 1981.

Brosseau, M., J. Knight, and John Witham. *Inventory of Railway Station Buildings in Canada*, Environment Canada, Parks Service, Ottawa.

Brown, Ron. *50 Unusual Things to See in Ontario*, Boston Mills Press, Erin, 1989.

Burnet, Robert G. 'Darlington and Port Union Stations', *Canadian Rail* 412, September/October, 1989.

Canadian Pacific Railway, Chief Engineers Office. *Standard Plans*, 1921.

'Toronto Union Station: History and Description', *Canadian Railway and Marine World*, 1927.

Cavalier, Julian. *North American Railroad Stations*, A.S. Barnes and Co., Cranbury NJ, 1979.

Chartrand, Guy. 'Les 100 ans de la Gare Windsor', *Canadian Rail* 408, January/Febuary, 1989.

Chevrier, Gilles. 'Le Chef de la Gare St-Lazare', *Canadian Rail* 236, September/October, 1970.

Collins, Robert. 'The Day the King Came to Moose Jaw' *Readers Digest*, March, 1973.

Conlin Engineering. *CN Railway Station Feasibility Study*, Town of Rainy River, 1988.

Coo, Bill. *Scenic Rail Guide to Central and Atlantic Canada*, Grey de Pencier Books, Toronto, 1983.

Coo, Bill. *Scenic Rail Guide to Western Canada*, 1982.

Cook, Clayton D. *End of the Line: the Pictorial History of the Newfoundland Railway*, Harry Cuff Publications Ltd., St. John's, 1989.

Cooper, Charles. *Narrow Gauge for Us*, Boston Mills Press, Erin, 1982.

Cooper Charles. *Rails to the Lakes*, Boston Mills Press, Erin, 1980.

Cooper, Juanita, 'Original Depot Hub of Hustle and Bustle', *Gravenhurst News*, Oct 1, 1986.

Corporation des Gares des Laurentides, Inc. *Inventiare des gares de la region des Laurentides*, MAC, Direction du patrimoine, Montreal, 1989.

Cote, Jean-G. 'Steam Hauled Silk Trains', *Canadian Rail* 293, November/December, 1974.

'CPR's Royal Train'. *Railway and Shipping World*, October, 1901.

Crichton V. *Pioneering in Northern Ontario*, Mika Publishing, Belleville, 1975.

Cruise, David and Alison Griffiths. *Lords of the Line*, Viking Penguin, Markham, 1989.

Curie, A.W. *The Grand Trunk Railway of Canada*, University of Toronto Press, Toronto, 1957.

Dalibard, Jacques, 'Getting on the Right Track', *Canadian Heritage* 10, 1984.

Davis, Jo, ed. *Not a Sentimental Journey: What's Behind the VIA Rail Cuts*, Gunbyfield Publishers, 1990.

Dempsey, Hugh A., ed. *The CPR West*, Douglas & McIntyre, Vancouver, 1985.

Denhez, Marc, 'Railway Blues: Stations are Coming Down in a Legal Vacuum', *Canadian Heritage* 41, 1983.

Denhez, Marc. *Heritage Fights Back*, Fitzhenry and Whiteside, Toronto, 1978.

Droege, John. *Passengers ,Terminals and Trains*, McGraw Hill, New York, 1916.

Eagle, John A. *The Canadian Pacific and the Development of West ern Canada, 1896-1914*, McGill-Queens Press, 1989.

Easton, Mel, 'Mel Easton's History of the K and P', *Perth Courier*, 1978.

Edmonson, H.A. and R.V. Francaviglin. *Railroad Station Planbook*, Kalmbach Books, Milwaukee, 1977.

Facts and Figures, Canadian Pacific Railway, 1937.

Ferguson, Ted. *Sentimental Journey: An Oral History of Train Travel*, Doubleday, Toronto, 1985.

Folkins, Wentworth, and Michael Bradley. *The Great Days of Canadian Steam: A Wentworth Folkins Portfolio*, Hounslow Press, Willowdale, 1988.

Folster, David, 'Why McAdam NB Has Such a Big Railway Station', *Canadian Geographic*, April/May, 1982.

Foran, Max, 'The CPR and the Urban West 1881-1930', in *The CPR West*, Hugh Dempsey ed., Douglas & McIntyre, Vancouver, 1985.

Garland, Aileen. 'Gardens Along the Right of Way', *Manitoba Pageant*, Winter 1977.

'The Future of the Railway Heritage', Royal Society of Arts — Cubitt Trust Panel, London, 1985.

Geddes, Hilda. *The Canadian Mississippi River*, Snow Road, Ontario, 1988.

Get Your Farm Home from the CPR, Canadian Pacific Railway, Department of Natural Resources, Calgary, 1915.

Graham, Allan. '"One Every Two and a Half Miles": A Brief Look at the Railway Stations on the Prince Edward Island Railway', *Canadian Rail* 382, September/October, 1984.

Grant, H.R., and Charles Bohi. *The Country Railroad Station in America*, Centre for Western Studies, Sioux Falls, North Dakota, 1988.

Gray, James H. *Red Lights on the Prairies*, Macmillan of Canada, 1971.

Groupe, Harcart. *Inventaire des gares du Canadien Pacifique de la region des Laurentides*, MAC, Direction du patrimoine, Montreal, 1989.

Hanna, D.B. *Trains of Recollection*, Macmillan, Toronto, 1924.

Hart, E.J. *The Selling of Canada*, Altitude Publishing, Banff, 1983.

Hart, E.J. 'See This World Before the Next', in *The CPR West*, Hugh Dempsey ed., Douglas & McIntyre, Vancouver, 1985.

Hedges, James B. *Building the Canadian West: Land Colonization Policies of the CPR*, Macmillan, 1939.

Heels, Charles. *Railroad Recollections*, Alan R. Capon ed., Museum Restoration Service, Bloomfield, 1980.

Holmes, Ed. *Life at the Keewatin Station*, manuscript.

Humphrey, Edythe. 'Station Agents Job Hectic in Nokomis of 1907', *Regina Leader Post*, December 31, 1955.

Hungry Wolf, Adolf and Okan. *Canadian Railway Stories*, Good Medicine Books, Skookumchuk, BC.

Jackson, John, and John Burtniak. *Railways in the Niagara Peninsula*, Mika Publishing, Belleville, 1978.

Jones, David C. *Empire of Dust*, University of Alberta Press, Edmonton, 1987.

Kalman, Harold. *Railway Hotels and the Development of the Chateau Style in Canada*, University of Victoria, Maltwood Studies in Architectural History, Volume 1, 1968.

Kalman, Harold. 'What to do with all those Redundant Stations', *Canadian Heritage*, December, 1980.

Kitigawa, M. *This is My Own: Letters to Wes and Other Writings on Japanese Canadians*, Talon Press, Vancouver, 1985.

Kozma, Leslie Steve. *A Building Survey and Brief Architectural and Graphic Examination of Railway Stations in Alberta*, Alberta Culture, Edmonton, 1976.

Kurelek, William and A. Isaacs. *Jewish Life in Canada*, Hurtig, Edmonton, 1985.

Lamb, W. Kaye. *History of the Canadian Pacific Railway*, Macmillan, Toronto, 1977.

Lampman, Archibald. 'The Railway Station', from *The Poems of Archibald Lampman*, ed. D.C. Scott, 1900.

Lavallee, Omer. 'The Saga of Barrington Station', *Canadian Rail*, December, 1965.

Lavallee, Omer. 'Windsor Station, 1889-1964', *Canadian Rail*, 1965.

Lavallee, Omer. *Van Horne's Road*, Railfare Enterprises, Toronto, 1974.

Laver, Ross. 'Board Orders Public Inquiry into CP Station Demolition', *Globe and Mail*, Nov 27, 1982.

'Downtown Facelift Should Preserve Station', *Regina Leader Post*, July 8, 1976.

Legget, Robert F. *Railways of Canada*, Douglas & McIntyre, Vancouver, 1973.

Les Amis de la Gare Windsor, *La Gare Windsor*, Montreal, 1973.

Leslie, Donald. *Donald Leslie Memoirs*, Glenbow Institute Archives, Calgary.

Liddell, Ken. *I'll Take the Train*, Western Producer Prairie Books, Saskatoon, 1977.

MacKay, Niall. *Over the Hills to Georgian Bay: A Picture History of the Ottawa Arnprior and Parry Sound Railway*, Boston Mills Press, Erin, 1081.

Marron, Kevin, "Preservation attempt destroys rail station", *The Globe and Mail*, January 1, 1988,

Marsh, Lon. 'The Edmonton Chamber of Commerce Friendship Train', *Canadian Rail* 402, January/Febuary, 1988.

Martin, J. Edward. *Railway Stations of Western Canada*, Studio E, White Rock BC, 1980.

McCombs, Arnold. 'The Agassiz Station', *Canadian Rail* 421, March/April, 1991.

McDougall, Terry. 'How We Won the Battle of the Railway Stations', *Canadian Heritage Magazine*, Winter, 1988.

McDougall, Terry. *Making Tracks, Thanks to Adrien Gregoire: Nine Country Stations Get a New Lease on Life*, Canadian Heritage, Summer, 1989.

Meeks, Carol. *The Railroad Station*, Yale University Press, New Haven, 1964.

McGregor, Don. '105th Anniversary of Railway YMCAs', YMCA Archives, Orillia, Ontario, 1985.

Mika, Nick and Helma, with Donald M. Wilson. *Illustrated History of Canadian Railways*, Mika Publishing, Belleville, 1986.

Moody, Howard G., 'ATCS Components Start Giving Results', *Modern Railroads*, March, 1990.

National Liberal Caucus. *Report of the Federal Liberal Task Force on Via Rail*, November, 1989.

National Register of Historic Places, U.S. Department of the Interior. *Historic Railroad Stations, A Selected Inventory*, Washington, D.C., 1974.

Neilson, Hugh. *The Diaries of Hugh Neilson, St. Catharines Station, 1861*. manuscript, Ontario Public Archives.

'New CPR Depot to be Opened This Month', *Edmonton Daily Bulletin*, Aug 2, 1913.

Newell, Dianne, and Ralph Greenhill. *Survivals: Aspects of Industrial Archaeology in Ontario*. Boston Mills Press, Erin, 1989.

'North Toronto Station, Canadian Pacific Railway', *Canadian Railway and Marine World*, August, 1915.

'Old Station Being Razed on 49th Anniversary of First Train', *Edmonton Journal*, Oct 20, 1951.

'Opening of New Canadian National Depot', *Edmonton Bulletin*, March 16, 1928.

O'Reilly, D. 'Historic Orangeveille Station Threatened', *Real Estate News*, March 9, 1984.

'Historic Train Station May be Saved', *Oshawa-Whitby This Week*, March 16, 1988.

Patrick, Calvin M. 'Early Railway Shipments of Canadian Livestock', *Canadian Rail* 407, November/December, 1988.

Pennington, Myles. *Railways and Other Ways*, Williamson and Company, Toronto, 1894.

Pictures from the Past, Muskoka Pioneer Village, **Huntsville**.

Planning for Heritage Railway Stations, Ontario Heritage Foundation, in cooperation with Canadian National Railways and VIA Rail, 2 volumes, Toronto, 1987.

Poirier, Daniel, 'Le P'tit Train du Nord', *Canadian Rail*.

Pope, Joseph. *The Tour of Their Royal Highnesses, the Duke and Duchess of Cornwall and York Through the Dominion of Canada in the Year 1901*. Ottawa, S.E. Dawson, 1903.

Public Archives of Canada, RG 46, Series C-11-1,, Volume 1415, File 11389.1, 1945, Station Plans.

Public Archives of Canada, RG 46, Series C-11-1, Vol 1415, File 8883.4, Telephones in Stations, 1909-1935.

Pubic Archives of Canada, RG 46, Series C-11-1, Vol 1448, File 17061, Closings of Stations on Weekends and Holidays, 1911-1961.

Public Archives of Canada, RG 46, Series C-11-1, Vol 1538, File 18540.25, Naming Railway Stations, part 1, 1916-1929; Part 2, 1931-1952.

Public Archives of Canada, RG 46, Series C-11-1, Vol 1526, File 10729, CP Standard Plans for Western Lines, 1929.

Public Archives of Canada, RG 12, Vol 1345, File 3350-3 History of Government Control and Regulation of Railways in Canada, 1891-1953.

Public Archives of Canada, RG 30 M ACC 78903/42, Grand Trunk Railway Station Plans.

Queen's University Archives, *1939 Royal Tour Scrapbook*, 2 volumes.

'Rail Station Demolition May Spark Man vs. Bulldozer Battle', *Edmonton Journal*, March 28, 1978.

A Railway Station Information Kit: An Aid for the Conservation of Heritage Railway Stations, Ontario Heritage Foundation, Toronto.

Railway Stations of Manitoba, Manitoba Ministry of Culture, Historic Resources Branch, 1986.

'Remembering: It was an event when the train came to town', special issue of *The Coupler*, BC Rail.

R.J. Long Consultants, Ltd. *CPR Station Redevelopment*, Town of Orangeville BIA, 1984.

Richards J., and John M MacKenzie. *The Railway Station, a Social History*, Oxford University Press, 1986.

Ross, Murray G. *The YMCA in Canada*, Ryerson Press, Toronto, 1951.

Ruel, A. and B. Salomon de Friedberg. *Les gares de chemins de fer au Quebec, Analyse typologique et selection*, Quebec, MAC, 1982.

'Saskatchewan Towns Finding Use for Empty Railway Stations', *Regina Leader Post*, February 8, 1978.

Sawchuck Peach Associates. *Cobalt Railway Station Feasibility Study*, Town of Cobalt, Sudbury, 1985.

Scrivener Leslie, and Jim Wilkes. 'Art's Too Late to save Historic Station', *Toronto Star*, Nov 25, 1982.

Smith, Doug. 'A Tale of Two Stations: Quebec's Palais Station', *Canadian Rail* 394, September/October, 1986.

Photos Historiques de Saguenay-Lac St Jean, Societe Historique de Sagueney.

'Society Wants CP Rail Buildings Saved', *North Bay Nugget*, November 10, 1987.

Spears, Tom, 'CP Denies Demolished Building was Station', *Toronto Star*, Dec 6, 1984.

Stamp Robert M. *Riding the Radials*, Boston Mills Press, Erin, 1989.

Stamp, Robert M. 'Steel of Empire: Royal Tours and the CPR', in *The CPR West*, Hugh Dempsey ed, Vancouver, 1985.

Stevens, G.R. *Canadian National Railways*, 2 vols, Clarke Irwin and Co., Toronto., 1962.

'Storming the Station', *Hamilton Spectator*, Dec 28, 1895.

A Study of Canadian Pacific's Heritage Railway Properties, Ontario Heritage Foundation, in cooperation with CP Rail and VIA Rail, Toronto, 1989.

Talman J. J., *Impact of the Railway on a Pioneer Community*, Canadian Historical Association, Ottawa, 1955.

Tatley, Richard. *Steamboat Era in the Muskokas*, 2 vols, Boston Mills, Erin, 1983.

Taylor, Sterling, 'Vintage Rail Station Back in King after 22 Years Away From Home', *Toronto Star*, Dec 15, 1989.

Thompson, Allan. 'Summerhill Station Slated For Yet Another Lease On Life', *Toronto Star*, May 29, 1990.

Thompson, John. 'Does the Original Champlain and St. Lawrence Station Exist?' *Canadian Rail* 395, Nov/Dec, 1986.

Town of White River. *The Birthplace of Winnie the Pooh: Our Discovery*, Information Kit, 1990.

Tozer, Ron and Dan Strickland. *A Pictorial History of Algonquin Park*, The Friends of Algonquin Park and the Ontario Ministry of Natural Resources, 1986.

Trout, J.M. and Edward. *The Railways of Canada for 1871*, Monetary Times, Toronto, 1871; reprinted, Coles Publishing Company, Toronto, 1970.

Walker, Frank N. *Four Whistles to Wood Up*, Upper Canada Railway Society, Toronto, 1953.

Vizralek, F., et al, 'North Dakota Railway Depots', *North Dakota History*, vol. 42, 1975.

Von Baeyer, E. *Rhetoric and Roses: a History of Canadian Gardening*, Fitzhenry and Whiteside, Markham, 1984.

Weaver, Martin E. 'Union Station Gets the Cinderella Treatment', *Canadian Heritage*, August/September, 1985.

Welcome to Station Park, promotional brochure, London, Ontario, 1990.

Willmot, Elizabeth. *Meet Me at the Station*, Gage Publishing, Toronto, 1976.

Willmot, Elizabeth. *Faces and Places Along the Railway*, Gage Publishing, Toronto, 1979.

Wilson, Dale. *Algoma Central Railway*, Nickel Belt Rails #4, Sudbury, 1984.

Wilson, Don, *Lost Horizons*, Mika Publishing, Belleville, 1986.

Wilson, Don. *Ontario and Quebec Railway*, Mika Publshing, Bellevile, 1984.

Withrow, W.H. *Our own Country*, Toronto, 1887.

Worthen S.S. 'Bonaventure Station, Montreal', *Canadian Rail* 293, November/December, 1974.

INDEX TO STATIONS

Printed in Canada